From Conflict
to Collaboration

From Conflict to Collaboration

A School Leader's Guide to Unleashing Conflict's Problem-Solving Power

Robert Feirsen
Seth Weitzman

THE SCHOOL SUPERINTENDENTS ASSOCIATION

ROWMAN & LITTLEFIELD
Lanham • Boulder • New York • London

Published by Rowman & Littlefield
An imprint of The Rowman & Littlefield Publishing Group, Inc.
4501 Forbes Boulevard, Suite 200, Lanham, Maryland 20706
www.rowman.com

86-90 Paul Street, London EC2A 4NE, United Kingdom

British Library Cataloguing in Publication Information Available

Library of Congress Cataloging-in-Publication Data

Names: Feirsen, Robert, 1951– author. | Weitzman, Seth, 1958– author.
Title: From conflict to collaboration : a school leader's guide to unleashing conflict's problem-solving power / Robert Feirsen, Seth Weitzman.
Description: Lanham, Maryland : Rowman & Littlefield, [2022] | Includes bibliographical references and index. | Summary: "The book is a 'how-to' guide identifying leadership characteristics and practical strategies that demonstrate how leaders can constructively channel a school's inevitable conflicts and instill a school culture that promotes group problem solving while honoring diverse voices"— Provided by publisher.
Identifiers: LCCN 2021055283 (print) | LCCN 2021055284 (ebook) | ISBN 9781475861723 (Cloth : acid-free paper) | ISBN 9781475861730 (Paperback : acid-free paper) | ISBN 9781475861747 (ePub)
Subjects: LCSH: Educational leadership. | Conflict management. | Group problem solving.
Classification: LCC LB2806 .F44 2022 (print) | LCC LB2806 (ebook) | DDC 371.2/011—dc23/eng/20220124
LC record available at https://lccn.loc.gov/2021055283
LC ebook record available at https://lccn.loc.gov/2021055284

♾™ The paper used in this publication meets the minimum requirements of American National Standard for Information Sciences—Permanence of Paper for Printed Library Materials, ANSI/NISO Z39.48-1992.

Rob: Dedicated with love to JoAnn, Nicole, and Stephanie, compassionate decision-makers all, who remind me every day of the value of understanding others and working for the greater good.

Seth: With boundless love for Jill, Jason, and Emily with the hope that our children will, as the coming pages suggest, find opportunity in the obstacles they encounter.

Rob and Seth: To educators everywhere who surmount challenges everyday with grace, courage, and a commitment to helping their school communities learn and grow.

Contents

Preface

We've noticed that in any informal gathering of school leaders, conversation ultimately turns to their job's challenges—as we imagine it does among any group of workers. Listening to administrators' gripes while on breaks at conferences or professional association meetings, we have found the subject is always the same: conflict. While the particulars vary, such as the controversial issue or the combative parties, there is a widespread feeling of being beset and under siege.

For a long time we assumed conflict in our own schools was the inevitable result of clashes between antagonistic people and opposing ideas. It took decades for us to grasp that the real problem was the underlying dynamic of how conflict is viewed and how it is addressed. In his third decade as a principal, Seth was on vacation and perusing the shelves of the Harvard Coop bookstore hoping to find a helpful book on leadership. That's when he spotted Mark Gerzon's book *Leading Through Conflict: How Successful Leaders Transform Differences Into Opportunities*.[1] Seth writes,

> Reading the title, I had a genuine epiphany. I instantly realized the fallacy of accepting conflict as an unavoidable and unenviable part of my job description.
>
> I proceeded to read volumes to learn how leaders in all types of organizations contend with conflict. I studied biographies of Nelson Mandela, the most amazing and accomplished peacemaker of my generation. These readings reformed my practice as a principal and transformed the school I led. Parent conferences were less contentious. Faculty began to repeat the language I was now using when faced with ideas different from my own. We were able to implement curriculum initiatives without the rancor that would have infected previous attempts. Once the most stressful bullet in my job description, new insights into conflict brought me together with faculty and parents as never before.

Rob adds,

Stephen Covey's[2] habit 5, "Seek first to understand, then to be understood," is one of the most important lessons I learned as a school leader. I've been both a building and district leader, and self-imposed pressure at both levels to make precisely "the right decision" when an issue arises is intense. Particularly in my early years in school administration, I felt that I had to demonstrate leadership by making on-the-spot decisions, which led to some outcomes that raised rather than lowered the temperature of everyone involved. Covey's recommendation requires that you take time to actively listen, something I didn't think I could afford. However, allowing yourself to engage others in meaningful conversation, to communicate an appreciation of their viewpoint, and to demonstrate empathy results in a better path for problem solving, even if it's a longer route. Once I changed my approach, my willingness to take time to understand resulted in less organizational—and personal—stress, a stronger sense of community, and decisions that had lasting impact.

We began writing *From Conflict to Collaboration: A School Leader's Guide to Unleashing Conflict's Problem-Solving Power* in the spring of 2020 during a divisive period in America perhaps unparalleled since the Civil War: protests rallying around the cry "Black Lives Matter" and sparked by the killing of George Floyd; controversy over wearing masks while the nation was mired in a deadly, rampant, public health crisis; a bitterly contentious presidential election eroding confidence in the American democratic experiment. We believe our interest in writing a book about conflict in schools was not coincidental given the national climate.

We also maintain that like our country, schools must engage in courageous conversations about the issues that keep us apart. Avoidance of conflict is not the cause of institutional racism and gaping inequities in U.S. schools but an unwillingness to confront the issues has enabled the status quo. Amanda Gorman said it best in her verse "The Hill We Climb" during the 2021 presidential inauguration: "We've learned that quiet isn't always peace."[3] Schools prefer to remain docked in calm waters rather than risk the stormy ocean of controversy. We attribute the problem, in large measure, to leaders' acute dearth of conflict-relevant skills.

From Conflict to Collaboration provides a framework for schools to find potency in conflict. This book will appeal to educators in public and private P–12 schools, candidates and instructors in school leadership preparation programs, and researchers examining school practices and leadership from the vantage of colleges and universities.

This book will often suggest specific *conflict-agility* language school leaders can employ. If there is any area of school leadership in which words matter, it is those delicate conversations that present an opportunity to either forge bonds or ratchet up dissension. "Yes, and" rather than "Yes, but"; "That's interesting, tell me more"; "We'll spend a few minutes looking backward but mostly we'll look ahead." Empathy and dialogue are the places where the proverbial rubber meets the road.

Scan the self-help shelves of any bookstore and you'll find plenty of titles including phrases like "Critical Conversations," "Crucial Conversations," and Difficult Conversations" that are indicative of the unease people feel and the potential for disastrous results. We highly recommend many of these books for school leaders, especially the classic *Getting to Yes: Negotiating Agreement Without Giving In*[4] and another multimillion-dollar best seller, *Crucial Conversations: Tools for Talking When Stakes Are High.*[5]

We confronted a question of word choice in writing this book: What exactly does a leader *do* about conflict? We found all of the verbs available somewhat wanting—perhaps a reflection of societal uncertainty about the challenges conflict presents. *Managing* conflict implies a degree of manipulation or a humdrum outcome. You often hear leaders say they *handle* conflict or *deal with* conflict, two terms carrying even more self-serving connotations. No one wants to be *managed*, *handled*, or *dealt with*. *Mediating* conflict has a specific meaning, referring to a dispute between two parties in which a trained negotiator intervenes to facilitate an agreement; this approach does not require outside help. *Resolving* conflict, one of the most common phrases, assumes a striving toward a Nirvana-type endpoint where conflict is forever banished. A similar term, *conflict resolution*, typically applies to programs that counsel students who are upset with each other as a way of helping them get along and avoid escalation. For lack of a better word and because *managing*, *mediating*, *resolving*, and their ilk all seem to miss the mark, we generally employ the term *addressing* conflict, which implies a willingness to examine conflict directly and assess options thoroughly.

Relying on the academic literature and the experience of its authors, we consider the role of the leader—whether a principal, assistant principal, curriculum director, department chair, grade leader, assistant superintendent, or superintendent—in fostering a constructive approach to conflict in schools, focusing on mindset, skills, and strategies. Adapted from the field of engineering, the process of *design thinking* is suggested as a method to devise solutions to complex, so-called wicked problems. *From Conflict to Collaboration* won't spell the end to differences but it can bring stakeholders together in search of common purpose and reduce the likelihood of conflict becoming an impediment to school improvement.

The preface begins the book with our personal experience; the last chapter, chapter 6, focuses on school culture and organizational vitality. This progression from the individual leader to the school community reflects our own journey as we confronted conflict and learned there is a better way. When we began to hear teachers repeat our conflict-agility language in parent conferences and collegial grade-level, department, and school meetings (for example, "Let's put blame aside. We're all responsible."), we began to understand the transformative power of conflict as a constructive and growth-inducing force. Guided by adept leaders, confronting differences without lingering discord is the first step for schools to come together and move forward on historically critical issues . . . and for our nation to do the same.

NOTES

1. Mark Gerzon, *Leading Through Conflict: How Successful Leaders Transform Differences Into Opportunities* (Boston: Harvard Business School Press, 2006).

2. Stephen R. Covey, *The 7 Habits of Highly Effective People: Restoring the Character Ethic* (New York: Free Press, 2004).

3. Amanda Gorman, "The Hill We Climb," poem delivered at presidential inauguration, Washington, DC, January 20, 2021.

4. Roger Fisher, William L. Ury, and Bruce Patton, *Getting to Yes: Negotiating Agreement Without Giving In*, 2nd ed. (New York: Penguin Books, 1991).

5. Kerry Patterson, Joseph Grenny, Ron McMillan, and Al Switzler, *Crucial Conversation: Tools for Talking When Stakes Are High* (New York: McMillan Books, 2012).

Foreword

Unlike that of most educators or educational leaders, my career has not followed a traditional path. I started my career in education as a special education teacher, worked in the corporate technology industry and higher education both locally and overseas and then eventually as a superintendent of schools in New York and president-elect of the American Association of School Administrators.

My unwavering passion for and conviction of the need for transformational change came from all of these experiences combined and from the lens of my children as they made their way through school and the requirements of corporate America. As someone with experience outside the field of education and a leader who has worked hard to help others see the need for transformational change, I am well aware of the need to manage and find alternatives to conflict in schools. As Feirsen and Weitzman explore as they discuss the process and ability to move from conflict to collaboration, strategies that engage others deeply in problem solving present the possibility of lasting transformational change in our school systems.

Education in the United States has remained stagnant for decades. Why? Many would agree that the greatest strength of our schools is also their greatest deterrent to change. Schools function best when relationships and culture within the environment are positive and trustworthy. Transformative change and progress are able to occur when there is an ability to question practice. Questioning that practice will inevitably bring conflict and dissonance. So when Rob Feirsen told me about his collaboration with Seth Weitzman on their book *Transforming Conflict in Schools*, I was intrigued.

Every day I see educators struggle as they work to do great things in their world. How do you struggle for positive change while you're maintaining positive, productive relationships with colleagues and meeting the requirements of outside entities? It takes a tremendous amount of courage to negotiate these relationships and requirements and experience the inevitable conflict. Feirsen and Weitzman's book provides an opportunity to understand the potential sources of conflict and offers guidance and a framework to move from conflict-volatility to what they term *conflict-agility*.

Whether you are a classroom teacher, building or district leader, or member of the governance structure of an educational organization, there is much to learn about how managing conflict in a productive and meaningful way can lead to powerful personal and organizational learning and transformation. In the current climate, it is imperative that everyone in education, particularly those in leadership positions, engage in practices that allow them to understand, manage, and grow in a difficult and politically charged climate.

Conflict is inevitable. Addressing and resolving conflict is essential in establishing a culture and climate that pave the way for continuous improvement and progress. Feirsen and Weitzman present a method to improve school culture and climate through problem solving and conflict resolution. This is essential if we are to move education forward and make our systems relevant and meaningful for current and future generations.

In support and collaboration,

Shari L. Camhi, EdD
Superintendent of Schools, Baldwin UFSD
President-Elect, AASA

Introduction

This book is intended for school leaders, scholars, and aspiring administrators interested in exploring an alternative approach to conflict in schools. The book begins with a foundation in academic literature before explaining a mindset and strategies useful to school leaders as they seek to resolve divisive issues that might otherwise thwart a school's pursuit of its vision and mission. Addressed constructively, the opportunity conflict presents to bring stakeholders together, examine their differences, and devise a constructive path forward renders it a powerful force for school improvement.

Chapter 1 describes the impact of conflict in schools: how conflict impinges on a school leader's day-to-day role and the corrosive effects on the school organization, relationships in the schoolhouse, and leaders themselves. The notion that conflict simultaneously holds the potential to remediate dissension in a lasting and productive way is introduced.

Chapter 2 summarizes research on conflict in schools. The chapter identifies social, psychological, and institutional sources of conflict as well as different conflict types. It highlights the competing pressures, open questions, and frequently unrecognized biases that provide fertile ground for discord. The chapter establishes a foundation for the model presented in the latter sections of the book.

Chapter 3 turns to the instrumental role of school leaders. On one hand, conflict is often attributed to school climate and combative interactions instigated by principals, superintendents, and other supervisors. On the other hand, leaders clearly play a pivotal role in ameliorating conflict by building trust, creating a mindset conducive to conflict-agility, and infusing their school's culture with a shared conception of conflict as an opportunity to collaborate and productively problem solve.

Chapter 4 introduces design thinking, a process derived from the field of engineering, as a framework to address the perplexing problems that lead to conflict. The chapter presents ground rules for school-community interaction and guiding principles for facilitating divergent thinking that can expand the universe of possible alternatives in conflict situations. Chapter 4 focuses on the empathize, define, and ideate stages of design thinking in which issues are studied and possible solutions devised. Proven protocols effective in schools are expounded, many of them derived from a considerable body of design thinking literature.

Chapter 5 continues our exploration of the design thinking process to demonstrate how conflicts are actually remedied. Whereas chapter 4 encourages divergent thinking, chapter 5 presents a convergent approach as schools implement and assess targeted solutions that recognize the contributions of all participants and address underlying differences in the values and beliefs that spawn conflict. Presenting realistic school situations, the chapter sets out strategies for getting unstuck when facing the thorniest conflicts.

Chapter 6 considers the capacity of conflict-agility to induce long-term organizational growth. By processing the process, the school gains insights into such pivotal questions as "How does a newfound level of conflict-agility enhance a school's capacity for critical school reform?" and "On this journey, what have stakeholders discovered about themselves?" The chapter envisions schools that rather than shun conflict welcome the opportunity conflict offers to build better schools with productive relationships and enhanced learning for all stakeholders—students, staff, and parents.

Chapters 1 through 5 conclude with a summary of the major points. The reader will also find follow-up questions designed to help him or her identify the relevance of each chapter's content for their own school. Chapters 2 through 5 also offer vignettes illustrating how dissension is manifest in actual schools. A pushpin symbol ⚐ calls attention to dozens of practical exercises you may employ to hone your school's conflict-agility.

School building and district leaders, including superintendents, district-level assistant superintendents and directors, principals, assistant principals, department and grade-level chairs, and team leaders will find this book an invaluable guide as they confront their most taxing challenges. The book might be suggested summer reading for an administrator beset by conflict. Superintendents and principals may plan book discussion groups with district and school leadership teams, taking advantage of the exercises at the end of each chapter.

Conflict is inevitable, as chapters 1 and 2 make clear. A productive approach to conflict confers benefits on almost every school, whether the level of dissension is dire or, as effective leaders often say, "There is room for improvement." Both school organizations and individual school leaders stand to benefit as the school adopts a healthier approach to conflict and a major source of administrator job dissatisfaction is ameliorated.

"The forest for the trees" metaphor potently applies to this book. The trees are pragmatic conflict remediation strategies, of which dozens are recommended in these pages. The book repeatedly points out that instituting these strategies effectively and consistently will ultimately reshape school culture—that's the forest in the analogy. Don't expect instant results, but as your stakeholders become accustomed to this new perspective, you will discover, as the title attests, conflict's problem-solving power.

Chapter One

Transforming Conflict in Schools

From Conflict-Volatility to Conflict-Agility

We don't get harmony when everybody sings the same note. Only notes that are different can harmonize.[1]

—Steve Goodier

School leaders harbor an idyllic notion of adult relationships in the school-house: teachers, principals, central office leaders, and parents amicably coalescing for the common good of the children they serve. Yet if we put aside oft-heard platitudes like "We are family" and "There's unity in our community," the reality is quite different. Conflict is always in a school's atmosphere, varying in degree from low-level smog to a full-blown toxic environment.

Conflict inevitably accompanies human interactions. While conflict takes many forms, it is broadly "a process that occurs when an individual or a group realizes that their interests are obstructed or negatively influenced by others."[2] According to this definition, conflict is ongoing rather than a solitary event. It involves more than one party, and like air quality, it can vary from day to day.

School principals feel the impact of conflict in a direct and often jarring way. An old joke characterizes the turbulent life of a school administrator: A parent rings the school secretary one morning: "Jamie won't be coming to school today. The teachers are mean. Nobody likes her." The secretary replies, "But Jamie has to come to school. She's the principal!"

There is an element of truth underlying the humor. A school leader's day frequently careens from one conflict to the next: parents arguing over the imposition of disciplinary consequences they deem unfair; disputes over grades purportedly undeserved because content was not taught or the child's learning needs were not adequately recognized; complaints that a homework routine consumes tear-filled hours every night . . . or that there isn't enough assigned; parents saying, "My child is bored" or "The teacher picks on my child."

Every school reform effort generates a backlash of parent protests mounted in PTA and board of education meetings, newspaper op-ed pieces, and social media posts. Examples of opposed reform include whole language (when parents assert the approach neglects phonics, grammar, and spelling—familiar topics in the classrooms they once inhabited) and Common Core Standards (sparking opt-out protests in which parents refuse to allow their children to sit for mandated standardized assessments).

Another major origin of administrator job stress is discord among faculty members: principals and teachers pitted against each other and internecine dissent among teachers. Children in the sandbox are not the only ones not playing nicely in school. A Canadian study highlighted the link between staff conflict and principal job satisfaction in a period marked by "work intensification" in the principal's office.[3] Among the adverse working conditions the authors correlated with low principal morale were disputes with unions, resistance to change, and a contentious political environment.

A 2019 Education Week Research Center survey ascertained "major source(s) of friction" in the teacher-principal relationship.[4] These sources, in order according to teachers, were student discipline (52 percent); schedules and duty assignments (24 and 21 percent, respectively); approaches to teaching and learning (21 percent); parent issues (19 percent); and supervisory feedback (17 percent). As further evidence of dissension, principals reported the same categories provoked conflict 33 to 71 percent *less* than teachers asserted (see table 1.1).

While the principal is the titular school leader, the position is more accurately described as middle management, mediating between high-status teachers expecting deference to their professional degree, union contracts,

Table 1.1. Major Sources of Conflict in Teacher-Principal Relationship.

Conflict Source	According to Teachers	According to Principals	Percentage Difference
Student Discipline	52%	24%	54%
Planning Period Timing/Scheduling	24%	14%	42%
Duty Assignments	21%	14%	33%
Instructional Philosophy	21%	9%	57%
Parents	19%	11%	42%
Principal Feedback	17%	5%	71%

Source: Education Week, "Principals, Here's How Teachers View You," October 16, 2019.

work rules, demands of parents who consider themselves entitled to services they pay for with their taxes, the authority of central office and local school boards, and state and federal mandates. These conflicts result in principals feeling beset by a lack of control, stress, and job dissatisfaction. Wang, Pollack, and Hauseman determined that "constant pressure to adopt new programs" was among the most significant causes of principal discontent.[5]

In a study jointly sponsored by the Learning Policy Institute (LPI) and the National Association of Secondary School Principals (NASSP), principals bemoaned a dearth of real decision-making authority.

> You take it from every angle, and you have some decision-making power in terms of which direction your school goes . . . but there's so much that gets cast down from above that you don't have a say in—where you're kind of the used car salesman, you have to sell it to your staff and make them think it's a great idea even if you don't agree with it.[6]

Principals interviewed in the LPI and NASSP study also identified accountability criteria as a significant cause of dissension. No Child Left Behind and Race to the Top required that standardized achievement measures receive primary weight in evaluating teachers, causing a mismatch in expectations between school building leaders and teachers within individual school buildings, between principals and central office administrators, and often between educators and community members supportive of the accountability movement.

Arguments proliferate over basic tenets of public education such as the influence of schools versus families (e.g., Who is responsible for learning outcomes?); fair use of data (What criteria should be used to evaluate educators?); and the very purpose of education (In terms of school outcomes, what is the relative importance of academic achievement versus development of the whole child?).

In *Conflict and the School Leader: Expert or Novice*, Johnson recorded one principal's observation that "30 to 40 percent of this job is preventing or dealing with conflict."[7] Principals may feel a kinship with other organizational leaders in this regard: it has been estimated that leaders typically spend 20 percent of their time in the workplace dealing with conflict or its aftermath.[8] Interviewing principals, Msila found "all of them stated that their . . . training never prepared them for conflict management."[9]

None of this research comes as a surprise to practicing principals. Observing classrooms, conferring with colleagues in school hallways and offices, or running faculty and teacher team meetings, school leaders confront staff resistance to the latest educational initiative that its opponents consider ill-conceived. A negative appraisal on a formal observation report or year-end evaluation can generate weeks of back-and-forth recrimination. Oft-heard faculty room grievances include an absence of administrative support in situations involving overbearing parents or student discipline infractions: "She didn't back me up" or "I sent the student to the office, but nothing happened."

Rancor among teachers during department and grade-level meetings stymie collaborative planning efforts. Principals and superintendents are accustomed to teachers nervously closing the door upon entering their office and slumping in a metal frame chair before confiding that a colleague is an impediment to productive group discussion.

A considerable number of principals feel disillusioned enough to leave their school and move on. The 2016 National Teacher and Principal Survey administered by the National Center for Education Statistics (NCES) found that out of 86,180 principals responding, 15.9 percent either somewhat agreed or strongly agreed with the statement "The stress and disappointments involved with being a principal at this school aren't really worth it."[10]

Even more concerning were the results of a follow-up study conducted a year later. Among those doubting whether their job was worth it, 13.3 percent had left the principalship entirely while another 7.5 percent had transferred to a different school. Twenty-nine percent of principals in the 2016 survey reported less enthusiasm for the job. Among this group a year later, 14.4 percent were no longer serving as principals while another 7.4 percent had changed schools. Although the NCES survey did not examine the source of the principals' dissatisfaction, it is not much of a leap to presume that incessant conflict was a common cause. It's just not what school leaders signed up for.

The sources of conflict in schools are wide ranging and often deep seated. Here are some examples.

Tracking: A suburban middle school confronts the issue of student placement in mathematics. Long-standing practice sorts seventh and eighth graders into stratified mathematics courses taught at remedial, on-grade, and advanced levels. A powerful lobby of parents argue their children will not be challenged without the opportunity to enroll in an accelerated curriculum. Administrator and teacher phones ring and inboxes fill with parental pleas when placement recommendations are revealed and parents realize their children were denied entry to upper-level courses. The school is immersed in dispute as parents appeal decisions up the chain of command.

While defending student decisions, ironically, faculty support for tracking is lukewarm. While some mathematics teachers believe that tracking enables teachers to differentiate curriculum and meet diverse learning needs, others are troubled by significant pitfalls. Children living in low income or recent immigrant households and children of color are overrepresented in remedial classes—partly an outcome of white, affluent, college-educated parents effectively pressuring school staff.[11] Differing positions are anchored in competing values, and when values are involved, tensions can rise rapidly.

The Union Rep Meeting: School leaders typically arrange meetings with teacher union representatives for the worthy purpose of airing and resolving mutual concerns. In the name of avoiding disagreeable surprises, an email might be circulated in advance requesting agenda items. The response is often a list of teachers' grievances about school administration: ineffectual student discipline, lack of backbone vis-à-vis parents, ill-conceived education reforms, poorly designed faculty meetings and professional development workshops, sinking morale . . . to name just a handful.

No one looks forward to these tense sessions, which manifest a predictable point-counterpoint pattern. Union officers level accusations raised by their membership followed by defensive administrators justifying their actions and decisions. Verbal grenades are tossed in both directions, one side accusing the other of incompetence, indifference, or defective character. "The student should have been suspended." "I'd like to walk out the door at three o'clock too." New complaints are raised each month or past grievances are recycled. From year to year there is little progress in modulating the discordant tone. If the faculty claims to be a family, it is a dysfunctional one.

Consequential Conversations, Race: A school counselor running a lunch-time club in his office momentarily steps out. While he is away, a white student raises the volume on his cellphone, playing a song that accents the n-word in each chorus. Interviewed by school administrators, the white student claims he innocently played the song not realizing its implications while three black students attest the word was intended as a racial epithet. According to the parents of one of the black students, school administrators accused his child of lying, failed to report the incident to them, and disregarded requests for a meeting of the minds among all the children and parents.

The controversy rapidly escalates when parents of the victim air their grievances in a televised board of education meeting, file a complaint with the U.S. Department of Education's Office for Civil Rights, post critical comments on a variety of social media, and organize community meetings and protests in which students and parents ultimately call for the resignation of the board president and superintendent of schools. The incident ultimately pits neighbor against neighbor in countless heated conversations.

Technophile vs. Technophobe: The precise role technology should play in the classroom remains in question. Some teachers, often supported by school leaders, are first adopters, eager to use the newest technology. Other colleagues teaching the same subject may see such practices as style over substance. Department and grade-level meetings become the setting for extended philosophical debate that never reaches closure. As ubiquitous as technology has become, there is no consensus among the school's influential stakeholders yet no possibility of ignoring the issue either.

Antipathy is one manifestation of conflict in schools. Another outcome is the opposite: schools sometimes develop a culture that presents a veneer of friendliness and collegiality to avoid substantive dialogue and dispute. A veteran superintendent once remarked, "Show me a school where they join hands at faculty meetings and sing Kumbaya, and I'll show you an underperforming school."

From this perspective, conflict is inevitable as staff wrestle with irresolvable issues. Is the primary purpose of schooling a liberal arts education or job readiness? Where to draw the line between a partnership with parents and deference to the faculty's professional expertise? Is punishment or restorative justice the most effective response to violations of the discipline code? What does it mean to promote diversity, equity, and inclusion?

There are multiple perspectives on and few definitive answers to these broad questions. One way to address the inevitable complexity of conflict is simply to pretend it doesn't exist: conflict can be evaded if there is no expectation of collaboration or consistency from one classroom to the next. Grade-level, department, and faculty meetings function smoothly, at least on the surface, if difficult conversations can be averted in the name of maintaining collegiality. But as in any relationship, unaddressed discord is like an ice cube in the freezer: it won't melt on its own, and holding on to it can spread a chill throughout.

Why are schools rife with conflict?

Schools are busy, complex places, and the temptation to reduce their complexity to an easily understood framework is compelling. An oft-heard explanation for conflict in schools attributes its persistence to psychological deficiencies: the school includes difficult people who act irrationally. According to this view, schools are mostly populated with logical, intelligent, right-minded people but there is a subset of recalcitrant actors lacking some or all of those desirable character traits. The norm would be cooperation and consensus if it were not for individuals exhibiting defective thinking, dysfunctional emotions, or inferior moral judgment.

This characterization might sound extreme but it is actually quite commonly heard when listening to adults in the school describe disputes. "The parent is emotionally unstable (or too emotionally involved)." "The principal doesn't really care about children, only career advancement." "The teacher's perspective is dumb." "So-and-so is just lazy." To the extent conflict arises from abnormal psychology, the role of the effective school leader is then to vacillate between debater and therapist as the situation warrants, either advocating a correct point of view or placating disruptive emotions.

A second common explanation of conflict in schools revolves around the adage "change is hard." Acolytes of change is hard claim a degree of sympathy for intransigence. After all, they say, prevailing school culture once sanctioned practices now viewed as outdated. Furthermore, they'll acknowledge that the pace of change has accelerated, adding to the challenge of adapting to new initiatives. Less charitably, they might characterize opposition as knee-jerk resistance from hardened people set in their ways. Conflict, from this perspective, is an inevitable and sometimes appropriate defense against new policies or initiatives that have yet to stand the test of time.

Such explanations are simplistic. Attributing conflict to cognitive or psychological deficits assumes that schools attract countless individuals who cannot reason effectively or who display personality disorders that prevent them from cooperating for the common good—or that something in the school environment induces such aberrant thinking and behavior. This outlook ignores the fact that schools require a tremendous level of cooperation and problem solving each day just to keep the school community functioning. In actuality, considerable consensus, rationality, and coordinated action exist even in the most stressful or divisive environments.

The association of conflict with change grasps only a part of the picture and captures it only at a superficial level. "Change is hard" can be a condescending statement. It's often used in a self-serving context, employed to justify why *I'm* right and *you're* wrong. The acceptance of the doctrine is divisive, separating the staff into bold activists embracing the future and timid reactionaries who reflexively turn their back on anything new. If change is hard, it is then reasonable for school leaders to approach it as an exercise in physics: what degree of force needs to be applied to overcome resistance? Such strategies rarely produce lasting improvement.

Yes, conflict and change seem to walk the halls of schools together . . . but not always. School reform regularly occurs without hardening into conflict. As noted scholar Larry Cuban points out, schools have evolved a great deal over time;[12] one would be hard-pressed to say that the schools of today are the same as schools of even a decade or two ago. Some noticeable changes, like the movement away from rote recitation in the classroom or the replacement of chalkboards with whiteboards, have taken place with relatively little turbulence.

Innovations also spread in uneven patterns: what was hard for one school to accomplish may be achieved much more easily in another. Success in detracking, for example, has a strong relationship to local circumstances.[13] Similar examples can be seen in the adoption of instructional technology.[14] Because the connection between change and conflict is not hard and fast, school leaders need a more nuanced understanding of the circumstances under which some initiatives develop into full-blown conflicts even as others garner energetic support.

This books offers a different perspective on the sources of conflict in schools, viewing the discussion through the eyes of the practitioner and blending academic theory and practice as experienced in the field. From this stance, conflict in schools arises from the interplay of several factors.

- A Focus on Children. Let's start with the most obvious and the most intractable source. The care of children, society's most cherished and vulnerable members, arouses strong feelings. Parents zealously advocate for their children in the genuine belief they are meeting their deep emotional and unique educational needs, molding their values, and ensuring a limitless future. Educators dedicate their work lives to an affection for young people and a belief in the transcendent importance of education. Everyone cares wholeheartedly about children—they're worth fighting for.
- Differences in Values. Many conflicts are at their base expressions of disparate values, including political ones. Values shape behavior toward others as well as our understanding of child development, teaching, learning, and the purposes of schooling. The debate over tracking in mathematics described earlier reflects this kind of contrast. Other examples include how to manage a classroom, the need for a core curriculum, how much involvement parents should have in curriculum, the role of school leadership, how to address individual student differences, and how to measure school success.
- A Lack of Universally Accepted Models. In medicine, physicians apply similar treatments to fighting infection, and the protocols are based on a strong consensus among practitioners and researchers. While educators, think tanks, politicians, and parents generally claim they know the remedy for America's education ills, there is no universally accepted standard of practice. Research can be found to substantiate almost any proposition. Changes in education swing from one approach to another, political winds shift, and dissent is ubiquitous.
  - o The Common Core Learning Standards provide a dramatic illustration. Of the forty-four states that originally adopted the Common Core State Standards Initiative, thirteen states (almost 30 percent) later repealed, replaced, or delayed implementation, and the law itself ultimately expired and was superseded by the Every Student Succeeds Act (ESSA).
  - o Student discipline provides another example. Zero tolerance dominated approaches to student discipline in the 1980s and 1990s but now has given way as a best practice to restorative justice, a philosophical realignment from strict rule enforcement to a more flexible relation-

ship-oriented, rehabilitative approach. A school principal's incredibly complex job requires extraordinary wisdom and dexterity to manage evolving educational verities.

- Questions About Allocation of Resources. Schools require substantial assets, whether money, materials, personnel, space, or time (perhaps the most precious resource of all). There never seem to be enough of such resources to satisfy all the demands from stakeholders, policy makers, and the community at large. Politics rears its head when decisions about budgeting, staffing, and supplies are viewed as a zero-sum game in which one position can gain ground only at the expense of the others.
    o Principals know that teacher schedules are a consistent source of friction; that squabbles over allocation of technology can erupt at almost any time; that fierce debates can pit funding for the arts against athletics; that school district priorities may constrain the development of faculty initiatives; that choices about how to use precious PTA donations may create division among neighbors; and that "diversity" has acquired many shades of meaning.
- Role and Responsibility Ambiguity. Despite their hierarchical, formal organization, schools operate with overlapping responsibilities in many domains. The principal runs the school but teachers control their classrooms. The traditional factory model does not account for the power teachers have to determine practice in the classroom, and many a dispute has arisen over who should determine what to teach, how subjects should be taught, and how student progress should be evaluated.
    o The value of working as a team to help students with behavior issues is well established, but where the roles of teachers, counselors, parents, and school administrators begin and end is elusive. An individual teacher's concern may be taken up by the union, transforming a workplace conversation into a grievance. District leaders may intervene in school affairs in efforts to create better alignment among schools, but principals can view such actions as disrupting relationships with their respective school communities.
- Cognition and Emotion. Thought and emotion work together to drive decision making, and the brain's capacity to manage them and all other processes in our bodies is truly a wonder. However, difficulties that arise as disagreements escalate can challenge the brain's ability to balance cognition and emotion to make the best choices. Taking the wrong path can intensify rather than reduce tensions and push opposing parties into deeper conflict.
- Communication Problems. George Bernard Shaw is widely purported to have observed, "The single biggest problem in communication is the illusion

that it has taken place."[15] Mental processing—cognition—is required to weigh the meaning and value of any form of communication, associate it with related ideas or actions, and store it for future retrieval. However, the hectic pace of schools and the constant barrage of sensory input makes the processing of information problematic and increases the potential for misinterpretation.

- o Formal channels of communication like grade-level leaders and committee chairs are not panaceas: details can be embellished or eliminated as communication passes from one person to another in a game of organizational telephone. Similarly, gossip and innuendo can cloud intended meanings. Schools also have a tendency to focus on the here-and-now, and anything that does not have immediate relevance may be filed away (figuratively or literally) for a future date that is soon forgotten.

- School Culture. Simply put, organizational culture is "the way we do things around here."[16] School culture evolves from the shared, deep-rooted assumptions and beliefs of organization members and provides the standards by which the environment in the school and the world outside the school are interpreted and judged. Elements of culture include values, ceremonies and routines, behavior norms, power networks, heroes, stories, and symbols.

  - o Culture defines what should and should not be done. It can be so embedded in daily life that its role in shaping behavior operates out of awareness. As multifaceted organizations, schools often include one or more subcultures, sometimes organized along department, grade level, or seniority lines. Conflicts can develop when cultural beliefs are violated or proposed changes challenge existing norms.

Conflict does not require malice to emerge; it can develop despite the best intentions of all involved. Principals wish that they could simply urge parents and school professionals to get along, amicably settle their differences, and remember they share a common goal to nurture and educate the precious children they all love. Yet no inspirational speech, however passionate and well reasoned, will eliminate disagreement, which all too frequently can deteriorate into rancor.

Lines are drawn in the sand when supposed colleagues or parent partners are seen as acting beyond their authority, violating cherished values, being unfair, or breaching standards of behavior. That's why it is certainly not uncommon to witness around schools, in neighborhood coffee shops, and on social media wholesale demonization of groups such as unionized teachers, who are seen as automatically opposed to school improvement; clueless administrators, who have been out of the classroom too long; and pushy parents vying to get their way. "We're all in this together" devolves into "It's us-versus-them."

This us-versus-them mindset raises the emotional stakes and creates win-or-lose outcomes since for one approach to be ascendant, the other must be subordinate. It is not enough to differ on substance. Instead, character and professionalism are called into question. Factions vie for power, cliques emerge, communication breaks down, people question the rights and responsibilities of students, parents, administrators, and school boards as conflict becomes dysfunctional and threatens the school's ability to carry out its mission. No wonder school leaders think of conflict in gloomy terms.

But alternatives exist. There are productive ways to manage strife.

The literature on conflict in organizations posits three basic ways to deal with conflict. We'll call them the 3 *A's*.

Avoidance seeks to minimize or ignore the dispute because it makes people uncomfortable. (Patrick Lencioni's best seller *The Five Dysfunctions of a Team: A Leadership Fable* ranked fear of conflict second on the list of maladaptive organizational dynamics.[17]) Overlooking dispute is tempting because it offers an emotional respite—at least in the short term. So conflict is ignored with an array of justifications too numerous to entirely list. "It's not the hill I want to die on," meaning "It's not that important to me." The frequently used statement "Let's agree to disagree" is, somewhat paradoxically, avoidance mixed with resolve. "We're not ready yet" provides a rationale for inaction that can stretch to forever.

To be clear, avoidance is not always unreasonable. Sometimes avoidance is a smart strategy if, for example, the issue is relatively minor or a new leader has not engendered sufficient trust. However, avoidance of conflict very often results in a lost opportunity to build capacity for improvement.

The second *A* strategy in conflict situations is *attack*. Faced with opposition, combatants prepare for battle. In the context of schools, the weapons of choice include threats, institutional punishment, resistance to change, and disparaging those holding different opinions. School staff often describe a work environment fraught with tension and antipathy.

The 2019 *Education Week Research Center* report cited above surveyed principals and teachers to determine the extent to which their perceptions of the supervision process were in sync.[18] Responding to the question "How would you rate the principal's contribution to your school's working and learning environment?" 30 percent of teachers characterized the environment as somewhat or completely negative.

The same study found discrepancies between teachers' and principals' perceptions of fairness in assigning schedules, establishing classroom duties, drawing up student rosters, and dealing with feedback. Crossfield and Bourne's research also unearthed stark contrasts between teachers and principals in their perceptions of the role school leaders play in causing interpersonal conflict, with teachers attributing the source of dissension to principals.[19]

For principals and other school leaders, the goal of the attack strategy is to obtain speedy results and enforce compliance. While school leaders might not be able to withhold salary or summarily terminate tenured staff, there are institutional incentives and disincentives at the principal's discretion such as extra-pay positions (for example, department chair, grade leader, extracurricular club sponsor, preferable class assignments, and last period off). Principals may also employ classic aggressive behavior such as raising their voice, using menacing body language, or flinging accusations to project power.

The third *A*, the constructive alternative for an organization, is *addressing* conflict by offering proven strategies that reduce strife while harnessing conflict in the service of improving educational outcomes and relationships in the schoolhouse. Conflict is inevitable and, yes, stressful and messy. However, it can represent not an organizational defect but an opportunity to make better decisions, empower the school community, encourage creativity, and strengthen relationships.

Armed with strategies that can guide conflict to productive ends, school leaders can *turn to* conflict rather than *turn away* from it. They can develop conflict-agility as opposed to conflict-volatility. Conflict-agility is equivalent to conditioning muscles in the gym: progress requires consistent attention and practice, and there are exercises in which schools can engage to promote fitness.

The perspective that conflict can have value may seem counterintuitive. Kowalski notes that classical organization theorists saw conflict as a destructive force that diminished efficiency or as "a pathology to be diagnosed and treated."[20] Uline, Tschannen-Moran, and Perez emphasize that people in organizations often suppress dissension because they worry about consequences and lack confidence in their ability to navigate conflict constructively.[21] Msila concludes that most leaders consider conflict in a negative light associated with anger, frustration, and stress, and by doing so, they fail to recognize the opportunity and invigorating energy that facing conflict can engender.[22]

The effects of unaddressed conflict are indeed deleterious. Incessant disputes exhaust a school's limited resources and energy. To the extent conflict is a win-lose or us-versus-them proposition, voices and perspectives worth hearing are excluded. Maybe this is one reason why school reform has been compared to a pendulum ticking back and forth as one group temporarily gains ascendancy over another. Since conflict is stressful, there is also potential for psychological and physiological harm.[23] Myriad stakeholders come away dissatisfied with their interactions in school. Mired in conflict, schools become incapable of learning and growing.

Conflict is an inexorable part of the school environment, the same as it is in any organization as large as a country or as small as a family. There will always be a bone of contention (an eighteen-century idiom referring to two dogs vying for a bone and neither willing to yield). The dispute could be debating national health insurance, deciding which partner will scrub tonight's dinner pots, imposing appropriate disciplinary consequences, or launching a new mathematics curriculum. Disputes will never abate, but how dissension is viewed and how differences are communicated—this is where a school community can begin to come together.

We've come to believe the supposed ideal state, an absence of conflict, is not even desirable. By addressing conflict, schools explore creative solutions, engage challenging issues such as equity and inclusion, reject us-versus-them politics resulting in winners and losers, and at the risk of overextending our toxic-environment metaphor, clear the air.

James Baldwin famously asserted, "Not everything that is faced can be changed, but nothing can be changed if it is not faced."[24] Schools need leaders who will not shirk or suppress conflict but will skillfully engender school culture that regards different voices and ideas. Like all growth opportunities, it requires both courage *and* humility, but it is the best way to realize a school's unbound potential.

CHAPTER SUMMARY

An atmosphere of discord can drain schools of energy, resources, and support. It can also cripple leadership and increase principal job dissatisfaction. School leaders frequently confront us-versus-them relationships, institutional resistance to change, silenced voices, and one-dimensional perspectives. There are multiple and often overlapping causes of conflict: differences in values, a lack of consensus on best practices, scarce resources, unclear roles, communication problems, the interplay between cognition and emotion, rigidity in school culture, and of course, the supreme value society places on children because they're worth fighting over.

Organizations facing dissent can employ three alternative strategies, known as the 3 *A's*: (1) Avoid contentious issues; (2) Attack by disparaging opponents, invoking threats, and imposing punishments; and (3) Address conflict, thus recognizing that conflict poses an opportunity to remedy a problematic situation with creative problem solving that truly engages faculty, staff, and community. Indeed, the most profound issues of our time concerning equity, inclusion, and diversity in America's schools have no hope of improvement unless we intelligently confront our conflicts.

CONTEMPLATING CONFLICT

Here are some questions for your consideration as you think about the contents of this chapter.

1. Imagine yourself an extraterrestrial who has been assigned to draw conclusions about life in your school. What are two or three topics causing discord that you would note in your report (e.g., "People in this school often argue about . . .")?
2. Everyone has resorted to the first *A*, avoidance, and we've all probably observed (or possibly engaged in) the second *A*, attack. Cite examples of these strategies that have taken place in your school setting. What were the results?
3. In your experience, which types of conflicts are the most difficult to remedy? Why?

NOTES

1. Goodier, "Bringing Harmony to Discord," Blogspot, October 3, 2008, http:// stevegoodier.blogspot.com/2008/10/bringing-harmony-to-discord.html.

2. Goksoy and Argon, "Conflicts at School and Their Impact on Teachers," *Journal of Education and Training* 4, no. 4 (April 2016): 197–205.

3. Wang, Pollock, and Hauseman, "School Principals' Job Satisfaction: The Effects of Work Intensification," *Canadian Journal of Educational Administration and Policy* 185 (2018): 73–90.

4. *Education Week*, "Principals, Here's How Teachers View You," October 16, 2019.

5. Wang, Pollack, and Hauseman, "School Principals' Job Satisfaction," 79.

6. Levin, Bradley, and Scott, *Principal Turnover: Insights from Current Principals* (Palo Alto, CA: Learning Policy Institute / Reston, VA: National Association of Secondary School Principals, 2019), https:/learningpolicyinstitute.org/product/nassp -principal-turnover-insights-brief, 7.

7. Johnson, "Conflict and the School Leader: Expert or Novice," www2.education .uiowa.edu/archives/jrel/spring03/Johnson_0204.htm, 1.

8. Chan, Huang, and Ng, "Managers' Conflict Management Styles and Employee Attitudinal Outcomes: The Mediating Role of Trust," *Asia Pacific Journal of Management* 25, no. 2 (March 28, 2007): 277.

9. Msila, "Conflict Management and School Leadership," *Journal of Communication* 3, no. 1 (July 2012): 28.

10. National Center for Education Statistics, "National Teacher and Principal Survey" (Washington, DC: U.S. Department of Education, 2018), https://nces.ed.gov/ surveys/ntps/tables/pfs1617_fl03_p1n.asp.

11. For a thorough treatment of this issue, read Diamond and Lewis, *Despite the Best Intentions: How Racial Inequality Thrives in Good Schools* (Oxford: Oxford University Press, 2015).

12. Cuban, "Why Change Is Often Confused with Reform: The Multilayered Curriculum," Larry Cuban on School Reform and Classroom Practice, November 19, 2018, https://larrycuban.wordpress.com/2018/12/19/why-change-is-often-confused-with-reform-the-multi-layered-curriculum/.

13. Rui, "Four Decades of Research on the Effects of Detracking Reform: Where Do We Stand?—A Systematic Review of the Evidence," 181.

14. Martines, "For Ed-Tech Success, Why Schools Use Technology Is Just as Important as How: A California School Group Refined Its Goals before Turning to an Ed-Tech Company."

15. Kenny, 'The Single Biggest Problem in Communication Is the Illusion That It Has Taken Place," *Irish Times*, November 9, www.irishtimes.com/culture/books/the-single-biggest-problem-in-communication-is-the-illusion-that-it-has-taken-place-1.4404586.

16. Martin, "That's 'The Way We Do Things Around Here': An Overview of Organizational Culture," *Electronic Journal of Academic and Special Librarianship* 7, no. 1 (2006), https://southernlibrarianship.icaap.org/content/v07n01/martin_m01.htm.

17. Lencioni, *The Five Dysfunctions of a Team: A Leadership Fable* (San Francisco: Jossey-Bass, 2002).

18. *Education Week*, "Principals, Here's How Teachers View You."

19. Crossfield and Bourne, "Management of Interpersonal Conflict Between Principals and Teachers in Selected Secondary Schools in Bermuda," *Insights of Anthropology* 2, no. 1 (February 24, 2018): 90–104.

20. Kowalski, *Effective Communication for District and School Administrators* (New York: Rowman & Littlefield, 2015), 153.

21. Uline, Tschannen-Moran, and Perez. "Constructive Conflict: How Controversy Can Contribute to School Improvement," *Teachers College Record* 105, no. 5 (June 2003): 782–815.

22. Msila, "Conflict Management and School Leadership."

23. National Institute of Mental Health Information Resource Center, "Five Things You Should Know about Stress" (Washington, DC: U.S. Department of Health and Human Services, 2019), www.nimh.nih.gov/health/publications/stress/.

24. Baldwin, "As Much Truth as One Can Bear," *New York Times*, January 14, 1962.

Chapter Two

What Is Conflict and
Why Is It So Pervasive?

Even when we do our very best to treat those close to us with utmost respect and understanding, conflict happens. That's life. That's human nature.[1]

—Sharon Salzberg

To begin our examination of the origins of conflict in schools, consider the three following situations.

Bea Sertin, a middle school principal, comes to her office and finds two irate parents waiting to see her. Ushering them to seats at a conference table, Bea can already tell that this will not be an easy conversation. It does not take long for the issue to emerge. "We've had it with that teacher!" exclaims one parent, a comment that receives an emphatic nod from the other. "This is the second child I've had in his class, and he never gives kids a chance. He just doesn't like kids, and he's constantly criticizing what they do."

"Why is he still teaching?" adds the second parent. "To tell you the truth, we don't like him either. He's very cold to kids, parents, everyone. We want something done."

Here's another situation. Two high school teachers engage each other in the teachers' lounge. Erika, a special educator, starts by asking social studies teacher Luis to find use-differentiated materials for students in his tenth grade class because the students she sees for academic support need materials more aligned with their reading levels. Luis counters by asserting that students shouldn't need so much handholding at the high school level. He argues, "If they can't keep up with the work in tenth grade, they shouldn't be in the class." Both teachers walk away from the conversation unsatisfied, each knowing the last word on the subject has not yet been uttered.

Finally, at a grade-level meeting called to address concerns about student achievement in mathematics, a third grade teacher argues that it is unfair to ask teachers to meet on a weekly basis to review formative assessment results. She tells the principal, "I'm overburdened already with all the emphasis on technology, never-ending emails from parents, constant interruptions from the office, and the needs of the kids in my class. With all due respect, I can do very well by taking that same time and using it to plan lessons. Let the math specialist do the analysis. She can let me know what she finds."

WHAT IS CONFLICT?

Each of these situations illustrates typical conflict situations school administrators confront. The word "conflict" itself is in such common use that its characteristics and connotations are often assumed to be uniformly understood. This is not the case. Some view conflict as an event, that is, conflict happens at a specific moment and has a finite beginning and end. Others see conflict as a process, one that gathers steam over time and evolves in ways that reflect its background or setting, the actors involved, and the forces that impact them.

Conflict can also be expressed as something intrapersonal or interpersonal: one might feel conflicted about whether to watch a favorite show on television or use the same time to exercise, for example. Alternatively, the word might describe the contentious situations to which Salzburg's quote at the start of this chapter refers. In the hectic world inhabited by educators, "conflict" is frequently used to describe a technical problem, like an issue with scheduling.

This book examines the impact of conflict on organizational life rather than internal, personal states. Chapter 1 defined conflict in the most general terms as "a process that occurs when an individual or a group realizes that their interests are obstructed or negatively influenced by others."[2] Ghaffar takes this definition one step further by asserting that conflict "necessitates change in at least one person in order for their engagement to continue and develop."[3]

Conflict therefore represents a social process in which differences in point of view are accompanied by an insistence on change in the actions of at least one of the parties involved. The fundamental demand for change, coupled with the persistence of the dispute over time, separates conflict from transient disagreement.[4] This book employs these basic yet critically important understandings as its foundation.

SOURCES OF CONFLICT IN SCHOOLS

It is productive to think of schools as systems, that is, organizations with a variety of interrelated parts that work together to accomplish a set of goals. All systems process inputs to produce outcomes intended to align with their goals. Feedback loops connect the various components to ensure that the organization's activities produce desired results.

OPEN SYSTEMS

Schools are furthermore a special type of system: an open system. In an open system, the organization engages in, and is dependent on, a continuous interactive process with its environment. The larger context within which the school is situated is thus essential to maintaining its status, function, and survival.[5]

As open systems, schools depend on the environment to provide the inputs associated with educating youth including students, government regulations, the labor of educators, supplies, and fiscal resources. Schools then perform various transformational operations—instruction through curricula most prominently—and create outputs including gains in student learning and, ultimately, graduates sent forth into the community.

Feedback plays an essential role in open systems, and schools are no exception. Feedback helps maintain organizational stability by providing a steady flow of information about the efficacy of processes and by facilitating needed adjustments. A school's success therefore relies a great deal on its ability to maintain productive relationships with stakeholders and adapt to changes in its environmental milieu.

Given the interdependence of schools with the environment, it is no surprise that clashes derived from competing or opposing values of stakeholders inevitably influence what goes on behind the schoolhouse doors. Frequently these battles take place in the political arena, manifested in squabbles over policy, curriculum, and school reform. Values controversies also energize interest groups and have a profound impact on school board election results and taxation and budget decisions. Educators are political beings just as much as any other group, and classroom walls have never been thick enough to insulate schools from political conflict.

Additionally, schools offer a sense of place, a home base for all the members of the school community, and therefore shape personal and group identity and the values and shared histories they represent. Conflicts can emerge when elements of those identities are threatened and stakeholders feel that their territory has suffered an encroachment. Consider the outcry that typically accompanies proposals to change mascots, grade organization (from a 6–8 middle school to a 4–8 intermediate school, for example), or school attendance zones.

Dynamics within school buildings provide fertile ground for disagreements to turn into full-blown conflict. Schools are composed of individuals from multiple generations, backgrounds, beliefs, and social networks; while they may have much in common, no two perspectives are exactly alike. Thus decision making in schools does not occur in a vacuum: values shape priorities. Seemingly innocuous decisions such as lunch schedules or the location of the copying machine can therefore become imbued with controversy.

Remember too that relationships within schools exist on multiple social levels (e.g., student-to-student, student-to-teacher, teacher-to-principal). All these interpersonal and bureaucratic arrangements must somehow be made to mesh in order to address environmental demands and fulfill the roles assigned to schools for educating and socializing the next generation. Institutional arrangements do not grant equal power to everyone. The clash of values and their associated perspectives at one point or another becomes inevitable.

In such a complex setting, it is also not surprising that both individual stakeholders and social groups exhibit diverse qualities, most of them rational but others not. Formal and informal groups abound, power is exerted and contested, and events occur that are both planned and unanticipated.[6] The daily mix of actors, actions, and internal and external resources makes every school—and every school day—wonderfully unique. On the other hand, it guarantees that competing perspectives and interests will arise.

EQUITY ISSUES

Schools are increasingly diverse. In 1995, 45 percent of American students attended schools in districts defined as diverse, that is, a district where no single demographic group made up more than 75 percent of the student body. By 2017, that figure had jumped to 66 percent, and the trend shows no sign of abating.[7] Diversity is not confined to ethnicity. Today's society includes a variety of family arrangements, social groups, spoken languages, and cultural representations.

Unquestionably, diversity offers compelling benefits to school communities. It enriches classroom life, builds understanding as students engage positively with peers from different cultures, promotes social-emotional growth, encourages a more comprehensive understanding of modern civic life, develops broad perspectives needed in a global economy where information flows without regard for national boundaries, and helps ensure the continued vitality of the larger community.

However, diversity also creates and reflects a multiplicity of values, beliefs, and norms that steer behavior and make it difficult to find common ground. Despite the traditional view of schools as melting pots where different social groups blend together and learn from each other, schools in the United States have also demonstrated a long and troubled history of mirroring divisions in the social fabric, a pattern that sadly persists today.[8]

The causes of the deep racial, ethnic, linguistic, gender-based, and cultural divides found in schools are numerous and stem from disturbing chapters of slavery, racism, segregation, inequality, and nativism in America's history.[9] A detailed discussion of their origins lies beyond the scope of this book. The tensions their collective legacy sparks, however, have vast potential for generating conflict.

For example, schools must always make decisions about the allocation of finite resources, and competition in the face of scarcity creates hardened divisions in which some seek to protect privilege through practices of exclusion. Controversies about gifted-and-talented and advanced placement programs, for example, often reveal such effects.[10] Participation in school decision making may similarly favor some groups more than others by policy or practice. Differences in backgrounds and socioeconomic status can limit opportunities for members of the school community to develop feelings of safety, belonging, and trust.[11]

Conflicts over inequitable treatment can also arise from educators' misunderstandings and lack of knowledge. In extremely diverse communities, it may be difficult for principals and staff to develop a sufficient depth of cultural competence in times of rapid demographic change.[12] In other cases, the lack of diversity among teachers and school leaders may deprive students and parents of role models who come from similar backgrounds.

Cultural divides separating school staff from the communities they serve can alienate students and families and create a mismatch between the experiences of community residents and "what the school wants them to do, how it wants them to view the world, and what its priorities are."[13] Such gaps can also lead to school-based decisions that reflect unintentional, but highly impactful, cognitive bias as the professionals impose stereotypes as ready explanations for behaviors that do not fit traditional patterns and thus create further distance between groups.[14]

The negative impacts described above do not necessarily arise from intentional acts. However, that does not mean that the consequences are not systemic. Principals and other school leaders often lack the training or perspective needed to address the pervasive nature of racism and discrimination, preferring an approach that can be described as "color blind" rather than "color-conscious."[15]

Immersed in the multiple disputes that arise on a daily basis, principals may view diversity as a source of problems rather than an opportunity for school improvement. As a result, they respond only on an ad hoc basis to individual issues. By doing so, they ignore the deeper, underlying issues that cause conflicts to reappear over and over again and they risk overlooking emerging discontent until full-blown crises shatter a superficial and fragile balance.

ORGANIZATIONAL CULTURE

While cultural issues in our society in general exert great influence on schools, organizational culture also plays a significant role in the origination of conflict by structuring the social relationships and actions of members of the school community. As mentioned in chapter 1, organizational culture may be succinctly described as "the way we do things around here."[16] Culture is composed of shared beliefs, values, and symbolic meanings. It provides a framework for interpreting a school's history and current well-being as well as for guiding how relationships are formed and sustained.

The values and beliefs serving as the foundation of school culture also guide "sensemaking," that is, how stakeholders interpret the voluminous information presented to them on a daily basis.[17] School culture defines what is acceptable and what is not, thereby enabling some actions while constraining others. Significantly, culture is so deeply rooted in the minds of organizational members that it operates out of awareness most of the time.

School culture exerts a profound influence on the manner in which proposed changes are greeted. Some schools, for example, exhibit "moving" cultures. These schools emphasize teachers-as-learners, establish meaningful priorities that focus on teaching, distribute leadership widely, encourage extensive teacher involvement in initiatives, and maintain a student-focused vision. Disagreements among stakeholders in these schools are accepted as part of the process of change. Although disputes sometimes boil over into full-blown conflict, bonds among stakeholders are not broken and good feelings prevail.[18]

"Stuck" cultures, as the name implies, are focused on maintaining the comfort of the status quo. They are inward-looking and individualistic rather than collaborative in their orientation to the work of teaching. Conflicts are less likely to result in productive resolutions that move the school forward and more likely to generate long-lasting ill will.[19]

Even in the best of schools, elements of organizational culture can create opportunities for conflicts to arise. Embedded in the shared notion of what schools should look like is typically a picture of what Tyack and Tobin call "the grammar of schooling."[20] The conceptualization includes classrooms organized by grade level or by clearly defined content areas, the Carnegie unit for high school credit, the design of the typical classroom, and letter or numerical grades. Although society has changed a great deal over the last one hundred years, the basic design of classrooms has evolved little, demonstrating the potency of cultural beliefs.

The strength of the grammar of schooling can also be seen in the manifold attempts of teachers to impose traditional classroom design, expectations, and procedures on the forms of remote instruction that emerged in the wake of the COVID-19 pandemic. Teachers were not alone: many students, parents, and school leaders voiced a sense of being adrift in uncharted waters.

Schools have similarly been dominated by a focus on "presentism," a perspective that considers short-term results as the highest priority—perhaps as a response to the unrelenting press of demands that accompany each day.[21] For most educators, there are never enough hours to address all their responsibilities. The daily grind of the school day drains physical and emotional energy and defines victory as making it to the final bell.

In this atmosphere, presentism can predispose stakeholders to oppose change simply in the name of "Enough is enough!" Proposals for school improvement may therefore produce conflict as part of a strategy seeking to preserve a fragile, but at least wearily accepted, state of affairs. Change agents themselves may be vilified. Systemic issues remain off the radar perhaps until the storm emerges in full force.

The existence of subcultures within school buildings complicates matters further. As noted earlier in this chapter, schools are complex, highly dynamic places where many activities take place simultaneously. The organizational structure of schools, combined with recurring patterns of interaction that take place across the school day, can give rise to cliquish subcultures with their own norms and beliefs. Few schools escape subculture divisiveness. Examples include

- At an elementary school faculty meeting, primary-grade teachers argue for a more child-centered discipline code while upper elementary-grade teachers demand one focused on consequences for misbehavior to "prepare students for middle school." (Similar heated discussions occur at the middle level in the name of readying students for high school.)
- A math or reading specialist confronts a general education teacher who opposes co-teaching.
- Parents at a middle school decry a new health curriculum because they believe it inappropriately broaches such sensitive topics as date rape and sexually transmitted disease.

- A high school science chair looks on in bewilderment as a dispute about department budgeting breaks out among chemistry, biology, and physics teachers.

In other enterprises, these conflicts would be addressed by administrative fiat or through the imposition of employee discipline—not so, generally, in schools.

Unlike some other organizations, schools are characterized by "loose coupling." In loosely coupled organizations, the lines of authority connecting one level of the organizational structure to another are weak and individuals or units operate in a semi-autonomous fashion.[22] The phenomenon may be best exemplified by the oft-repeated statement "I do what I want once I close the classroom door." Loose coupling limits what principals and other supervisors can control and empowers stakeholders to take stands or exhibit behavior contrary to established goals or sanctioned practices.

THE ROLE OF TRUST

School culture and trust are closely related. A culture that stresses inclusivity, values input from stakeholders, and supports the sharing of experiences builds trust, which in turn creates a climate of tolerance for dissenting opinions and a willingness to accept critical viewpoints without defensiveness or negativity.[23] Trusting relationships promote cohesiveness and a sense that the different roles played by school stakeholders and the myriad activities taking place each day are aligned with shared goals.

Trust encourages members of the school community to learn from each other.[24] In schools with high trust, ideas about effective teaching strategies or useful materials are shared across the lunch table, feedback from the PTA is given thoughtful consideration, and principal walkthroughs are treated as a matter of course. In contrast, the absence of trust encourages wariness, limits expressions of empathy, and impedes clear communication.

Schools without trust may focus more on individual needs than organizational growth. The absence of trust builds barriers and diverts attention from issues confronting the school to questions about others' motives.[25] Gossip flourishes in schools with trust deficiencies as people fill gaps in knowledge with conjectures about secret alliances and the reasons behind decisions. Similarly a lack of trust contributes to hardened boundaries among students, parents, staff, and administration—a perspective that inhibits joint efforts. In short, trusting cultures build problem-solving capacity while cultures without trust leave schools open to recurring bouts of conflict.

DISAGREEMENT ABOUT BEST PRACTICES

Disagreements about best practices create additional sources of friction in schools. Conflicting schools of thought on teaching and learning compete for dominance in educational circles, and debates over the effectiveness of classroom strategies proliferate.[26] Consider learning styles, for example. Research has failed to show significant impact on student achievement but the topic remains highly popular in the field.[27]

Differences similarly exist concerning the best approach to classroom management and student discipline with one end of the continuum proposing restorative practices that aim for social-emotional growth and the other end advocating strict consequences for student infractions founded on principles of behavior modification.[28] Consensus on grading practices remains elusive, with views on the topic reflecting a wide diversity of opinion that ranges from a commitment to traditional single letter or numerical grades to advocacy for a multifaceted system that evaluates student work products, work processes, and progress.[29]

Debates about best practice do not spare school leadership. Many approaches to leadership have their origins in Douglas McGregor's dichotomous Theory X versus Theory Y characterization of worker motivation. Each conceptualization results in a different vision of leadership in general and supervision in particular.

Theory X postulates that managers cannot expect employees to be intrinsically motivated by the tasks set before them; instead, employees need to be directed and closely supervised. Theory Y, in contrast, asserts that employee motivation can flow directly from the work to be performed when roles provide opportunities for productive contributions to the organization. A related model, developed by William Ouchi, Theory Z, focuses on the value of a team approach to decision making and the importance of leadership in creating a culture of collaboration.[30]

Discussion in professional circles and research on school leadership styles reflect the influence of these different theories. Transactional leadership places the onus on supervisors to exercise authority, make tasks clear, offer rewards for compliance or penalties for poor performance, and closely supervise staff. Leaders and followers engage in trade-offs, or transactions, in which benefits are provided to employees in exchange for their completion of assigned tasks.

Transformational leadership, a style identified by political scientist James MacGregor Burns, is more aligned with Theory Y and Theory Z. Transformational leaders perform their role by empowering stakeholders in ways that satisfy personal needs for self-efficacy and self-actualization through collaborative processes of visioning, shared decision making, and building organizational capacity.

Advocates of a third style, situational leadership, emphasize the need for flexibility: leaders select strategies based on an assessment of the staff's level of competence to accomplish a given task.[31] A fourth style, instructional leadership, directs the principal's attention to the mission of improving curriculum and instruction with less emphasis on other aspects of school operation.[32]

As with questions related to teaching and learning, consensus about best leadership practices has proved elusive. The lack of consensus increases the potential for discord to get out of hand because absent a definitive leadership model, school administrators of all stripes lack guidance on how to proceed when conflict arises.

BLURRED ROLES AND RESPONSIBILITIES

Ambiguity over roles and responsibilities within schools contribute to the development of conflict as well. As previously noted, loose coupling places severe restrictions on administrative prerogatives. In addition, regulations, mandates, and the directives of supervisors may be interpreted differently by stakeholders, resulting in varying levels of compliance and difficulty in implementing school initiatives with fidelity.[33] Many aspects of instruction and student behavior management require coordination but the structure of schools and differences in beliefs about effective practice mitigate against interdependence and consistent cooperation.

Union grievance mechanisms similarly limit the options of principals and other school leaders, applying the brakes to leadership efforts to bring about change by challenging proposals that alter working conditions or job descriptions. The growing interest in teacher leadership promotes faculty engagement in substantive issues related to teaching, learning, and school governance but also leads to questions about professional responsibilities and accountability: Is the principal bound by faculty opinions or does the principal render ultimate authority? Who is accountable when plans go awry? When is it time to stop seeking input and call the question?

Principals themselves often experience similar difficulties in their relationships with the district office. Overlapping domains of influence and authority complicate decision making and create grounds for conflict: Who is responsible for making decisions about the implementation of a district-wide reading program? Is it the district reading coordinator? A committee? The principal? Principals may also be constrained in their ability to adapt district mandates to their individual schools with limited authority to permit options when teachers seek flexibility for what are perceived as unique or extenuating circumstances in their classrooms.

RESOURCE ALLOCATION

Most schools struggle with providing the resources required to address all the needs of their students. School boards and school leaders must continuously make difficult decisions among competing priorities for additional staffing, new or updated technology, instructional materials and supplies, physical plant repairs, professional development, and better wages and working conditions for employees. The need for increased attention to safety due to the COVID-19 pandemic and the threat of school shootings has only added to the challenge.

Individual schools themselves have limited control over the resources given to them to address the needs of the students they serve. Dependent on school districts or other central authorities for funding, schools rarely, if ever, receive the full allocations requested. Funding shortfalls inexorably affect school operations because virtually everything schools do involve the expenditure of money at some point.

The scarcity of needed resources inspires competition for attention from decision makers and provokes squabbling that can easily escalate into conflict.[34] Participants in recurrent budget or staffing debates come to view the decision-making process as a zero-sum game in which they can gain what they need only at the expense of colleagues, peers, or other members of the school community.[35] Decisions about the way staff, materials, supplies, and even time are allotted reflect institutional power arrangements that can deepen divides.

COMMUNICATION CHALLENGES

Conflicts also emerge as a result of unclear or misinterpreted communications. Directives frequently must pass through bureaucratic layers with each stop adding its own wording, emphasis, or interpretation to the original intended meaning.[36] Even explicitly worded mandates from the federal or state government or the district office are subject to diverse interpretations as stakeholders make meaning based on prior knowledge, individual school context, and discussions in their social networks.[37] The potential for distortion is amplified by the phenomenon of loose coupling, which allows for variation in implementation and moderates potential penalties for noncompliance.

Robert Ramsey, an author who has written extensively on the subject of communication in schools, identifies an overreliance on jargon as one of the common causes of miscommunication.[38] Educators, like other professionals, use specialized vocabulary terms to represent situations, activities, and artifacts specific to the field, including a great many acronyms. However, the terminology is not necessarily understood by students, parents, and community members at large.

Even among educators themselves, terms used by some groups or in some settings or jurisdictions may not have clear meaning in others. One need look only as far as the many ways schools currently identify students who come from households where the dominant language is not English (ESL, ENL, ELL, among others) to witness this phenomenon.

Ramsey similarly notes the tendency among educators to avoid delivering bad news: softer or misleading language substitutes for clear content.[39] An assistant principal once wrote an email to parents after a field trip that stated, "Students became so excited by what they saw in the first exhibit that the chaperones decided they should return to the classroom to explore the topic more deeply"; the school group had actually been asked to leave by the docent because of misbehavior.

In much the same manner, teachers who have been observed in the classroom by supervisors are well-acquainted with the sandwich approach to feedback in which a criticism is carefully layered between two positive statements. While this strategy may guard against wounded feelings, it represents the educational equivalent of burying the lede in journalism, cloaking in vague language the comments most relevant to improving deficiencies while evading the issue that needs to be addressed.

COGNITION AND EMOTION

The human brain is a marvelous organ but its operations can contribute to an escalation of debate to full-fledged conflict. Our brains enabled us to survive and thrive even under the most challenging prehistoric conditions and continue to do so under all the stresses of modern life. However, the brain's abilities are not limitless.

Like other organs, the brain needs a constant supply of energy: studies show that physiological restrictions on the amount of energy the body can deliver serve as a major constraint on the brain's ability to process information.[40] Working memory, the brain's system that holds information and makes it available for processing, has significant limitations as well.[41] These two factors have considerable influence on overall brain function and particularly on decision making under stress. Despite its deeply complex organization and ability to monitor many activities at one time, the brain nevertheless is a limited capacity processor.

The brain attempts to compensate for its limitations. Generally it tries to minimize social threats.[42] It has also become extremely adept at recognizing patterns. Capacity for pattern identification makes it easier to process stimuli and integrate functions across parts of the brain. Skillful pattern recognition allows the brain to compare present and past experiences, find matches, and fill in the blanks that are missing in order to speed judgment and then take action.[43]

Prowess in pattern recognition can be a double-edged sword, however. At times the brain may take shortcuts and make judgments on incomplete data, perceiving patterns when none exist. Cognitive bias, previously mentioned in connection with issues with diversity, represents one such mental shortcut. It may be defined as "a strong, preconceived notion of someone or something, based on information we have, perceive to have, or lack."[44]

Table 2.1 presents a summary of several cognitive biases of particular relevance to the subject of conflict because they can lead to inaccurate judgments and an unwillingness to consider all factors.

The brain is also the seat of our emotions, and emotions play a huge role when disputes arise. Emotions drive attention and thus help our brain distinguish between stimuli that demand notice and those that can be ignored.

Table 2.1. Cognitive Biases

Cognitive Bias	Description
Fundamental attribution error	Consequences resulting from an event are caused by an individual's actions rather than situational factors.
Hostile attribution bias	Those who disagree with you have bad intentions.
Normalcy bias	Things are most likely to continue just as they have in the past.
Confirmation bias	One's own explanations of phenomena are more likely to be accurate than those of others, making it easier to accept evidence that supports one's views and discount any dissonant information.
In-group bias	Encourages belief in those who belong to the same social group.
Anchoring effect	Focuses attention on the first piece of information encountered in a situation (particularly if that information is presented as a number).
Dunning-Kruger Effect	Reduces complicated ideas or events to simplistic explanations when foundational knowledge about the subject is wanting.

"Emotional tags" connect perceived patterns in the environment to our feelings; they can help us determine which environmental stimuli hold the greatest import and thus help us make quick decisions.

As with cognitive shortcuts, however, our emotions can lead us astray. Emotional tags can mislead us by enabling feelings connected to a given situation—perhaps allegiance to a social group like a grade level, department, or circle of colleagues—to overwhelm other aspects worthy of consideration like impact on a school as a whole. Emotional tags also can be attached to faulty prejudgments generated by cognitive bias, deepening a commitment to a given decision or course of action when flexibility might be more prudent.[45]

On any given day, schools witness expressions of joy, pride, and love as well as anger, jealousy, loneliness, and all the other feelings that characterize the human condition. Emotional temperatures can easily spike as disagreements escalate into conflicts, increasing stress levels and hastening a fight-or-flight reaction that reduces the capacity for reflective thought.[46] At the group level, emotions can lead to hardening of positions, loss of trust, withdrawal from involvement in the issues a school confronts, or an unwillingness to plan for the future.[47]

In short, cognition and emotion play pivotal roles in the way conflict is addressed. On the positive side, the brain can swiftly process information to identify emerging concerns, build productive, trusting relationships, drive attention to focus on the most important aspects of an issue, and provide the motivation for sustained commitment for personal and group efforts toward resolution. At times, however, mental shortcuts can lead to inaccurate conclusions, and stress can create a predisposition toward action rather than contemplation. Heightened emotions can similarly escalate tensions, encourage intransigence, and alienate potential allies.

If history is to be our guide, it demonstrates that relying solely on our brain power to address conflict does not suffice.

IT'S ALL ABOUT CHILDREN

Finally, the fact that schools serve children adds special importance and urgency to discussions about what happens within classrooms and school buildings. As President John F. Kennedy remarked, "Children are the world's most valuable resource and its best hope for the future."[48]

No one doubts the necessity for taking special care of students. Parents recognize that their children will spend approximately 1,100 hours each year, or 14,300 hours over thirteen years, in school and they want to feel confident that schools will provide the safety, nurturance, and skillful instruction that will lead to a productive and meaningful future. Research consistently cites the value of parent involvement in their children's schooling,[49] and organizations ranging from the National PTA[50] to the Centers for Disease Control and Prevention[51] emphasize partnership between school and parents.

For educators, the goal of making a difference in the lives of children serves as the motivating principle, or what school improvement expert Michael Fullan calls "the moral purpose" of their professional identity.[52] With emotional investment at high levels, it is little wonder that conflict is endemic to schools.

TYPES OF CONFLICT

A subject as complex as conflict has produced a good number of efforts to classify its various expressions. One approach considers the participants involved and their allegiances as most important. Thus a conflict may be interpersonal, intragroup (as within a particular grade level or department), or interorganizational (as when there are issues between the faculty union and the PTA).[53] Another model posits six different forms of conflict: affective conflict, substantive conflict, conflict of interest, conflict of values, goal conflict, and realistic and nonrealistic conflict.[54]

While these groupings have value, the conceptualization presented by Jehn captures in straightforward terms the types of conflict manifested in schools. It also provides school leaders with a foundation for selecting strategies to address them. Three conflict types are identified.[55]

The first type, relationship conflict, is familiar to all: no school exists that cannot report examples of relationship conflicts whether they occur in the hallways between classes, at social gatherings of the faculty and staff, in meetings with administrators, or in the interactions between parents (and students) and teachers. Middle school principal Bea, featured in the anecdote that started this chapter, heard about a relationship conflict in strident terms when she met with parents upset with a teacher.

The second type, task conflict, focuses on jobs, duties, or organizational functions that should be accomplished. In schools, task conflicts may address topics that include curriculum design, student assessment, bus schedules, or communication with parents. The confrontation between the special educator and the general education teacher discussed in the chapter's second anecdote exemplifies this type of dispute.

Process conflicts represent Jehn's third category. Whereas task conflicts address the what of an issue, process conflicts focus on who and how. The third anecdote at the start of the chapter, the case in which a classroom teacher objected to being asked to analyze formative assessment results, illustrates this type of conflict. The teacher in question does not argue about the work itself but rather who will perform it.

Disputes about process occupy a great deal of time and energy in schools: there is often a general agreement about purposes, but debate ensues when decisions must be made about how the goal will be accomplished, how resources will be deployed to support it, and to whom accountability will be delegated. Jehn concludes that high levels of process conflict can have a damaging impact on the performance of an organization by creating management issues for leadership and by promoting misalignments between ends and means that hamper everyday functioning and goal attainment.

Research suggests that people are most apt to associate conflict with relationship issues and to focus on the particulars that led to such interpersonal disputes rather than the quest for solving them.[56] It is also important to note that the three conflict categories are not mutually exclusive.

For example, a task conflict may be entwined in the minds of the participants with a process conflict as when a discussion about finding better ways to cement relationships with parents arouses concerns about how much more time this will occupy in an already overcrowded school day. Similarly, a process-oriented discussion of professional learning community (PLC) responsibilities may bring simmering relationship issues to a boil. Scheduling changes can lead to all three types of conflict as clashes emerge over union contracts, timetables for implementation, and whether the new schedule favors one group of teachers over another.

Sometimes a conflict of one type may masquerade as another. Principals may encounter this phenomenon when they meet with teachers or union representatives ostensibly to resolve differences about a new curriculum initiative—a task conflict. In discussion, they discover that the underlying issue is not the task of curriculum improvement but rather an unwillingness to change teaching strategies—a process conflict.

People may also interpret a conflict situation differently depending on personal or organizational history, interpersonal relationships, and professional roles. Department chairs, for example, may view a question of how to best use technology as a task issue (What is the optimal way to raise student performance levels through technology?). In contrast, teachers may see the question as a process concern (How will I find the time to master these new ways of delivering instruction?). As previously noted, emotions accompany decision making, meaning that almost any conflict can become a relationship conflict if tensions persist.

THE TWO SIDES OF CONFLICT

Regardless of its origin or form, conflict in organizations in general—and schools in particular—can be viewed from two very different perspectives. Traditional views of conflict emphasize its negative impact on interpersonal relationships, organizational culture, and organizational performance. As Bacal observes, "We tend to think about conflict as unpleasant, counterproductive, and time consuming."[57]

Considered from this point of view, keeping the peace assumes a high priority: group norms should discourage airing of disputes to the greatest extent possible. Leadership, in turn, should be evaluated on how well tranquility is maintained among stakeholders with any failure to contain conflict signaling management deficiencies.

Advice to leaders in this regard is encountered in oft-heard adages including "If you can't say something nice, don't say anything at all" and "Let sleeping dogs lie" as well as a stated preference for "smooth sailing."[58] Guidance of this type is not entirely unwarranted as teachers experiencing conflict report feelings of disappointment, jealousy, anger, and even sorrow with a resulting decrease in morale and motivation.[59]

Alternative views present conflict in a much different light—that is, not as an aberration but rather as an accepted part of our social lives, particularly our lives in organizations. Tuckman's well-known description of team development, for example, identifies four stages of evolution: forming, storming, norming, and performing and asserts that the second stage can include a high degree of discord that ultimately leads to group cohesion and impact.[60]

Contemporary perspectives similarly envision conflict as opportunity: conflict serves as a call to action that can lead to higher levels of organizational performance. In schools, conflict focuses attention on tasks and processes that need improvement while promoting productive—although often uncomfortable—communication among individuals and groups. It ultimately strengthens social bonds and facilitates the inclusion of diverse voices to create a more inclusive community, improve decision making, and propel a school forward in the face of challenges that heretofore seemed stultifying.

Addressed adroitly, conflict can be a source for good. Principals and other school leaders do not have to relish the possibility that disagreements can escalate into conflict, but they need not fear it either. As Isabu concludes, "When an organisation has an optimum level of conflict, organisational effectiveness is likely to increase."[61]

Despite the potential for harnessing conflict in the service of school improvement, school leadership preparation programs rarely provide training in how to address conflict. New principals find themselves unsure of how to respond when disputes erupt.[62] They are not alone; in fact, both novice and veteran principals feel frustrated and alarmed by the continuing stream of demands and complaints they face from all quarters.[63] Stress can result in the use of ineffective strategies that exacerbate rather than abate conflict and diminish the standing of school leaders in the eyes of their communities.

On the other hand, skillful leadership can enable schools to work through conflict on the path to school improvement. Over time, school leaders who develop conflict-agility can promote team effectiveness, cement trust throughout the school community, increase job satisfaction, clarify goals, and build the culture and capacity needed for an open system like a school to thrive in a changing environment.[64] The role of leadership in the development of the capacity to address conflict is the topic of the next chapter.

CHAPTER SUMMARY

To the layperson, the work of schools may seem pretty straightforward: teachers provide instruction, students learn, and school leaders and other staff do everything else. Educators know better. Schools are in fact open systems that conduct many activities simultaneously, have multiple stakeholders, and respond to frequently changing demands from internal and external forces. They are dependent on maintaining productive relationships with their environments. As a result, schools cannot avoid conflict.

Conflict can inflict great stress on a school. Specific sources include politics, competition for limited resources, loose coupling, organizational culture, disagreements about roles and best practices, poor communication, cognitive bias, and the emotionality that often obscures opportunities to bridge gaps between disagreeing parties. The fact that schools shape the lives of children adds a sense of urgency to many issues, and the impact of our nation's pervasive inequities breeds challenges and tensions that exacerbate debate and amplify rifts among members of the school community.

A model offered by Jehn identifies three types of conflict.[65] Relationship conflict is the type perhaps most familiar; it would be hard to find anyone who has never experienced any interpersonal difficulties. Task conflict focuses on specific organizational functions and activities. Process conflict addresses the steps taken to accomplish such functions and activities. The categories are not mutually exclusive, and any one of them can incorporate aspects of the remaining two. Whatever its form, conflict can present a threat to the stability and health of the school but it also can offer an opportunity to raise levels of performance and promote continuous improvement.

CONTEMPLATING CONFLICT

Here are some questions for your consideration as you think about the contents of this chapter.

1. Reflect upon a conflict you've experienced at school. Which of the factors discussed in the chapter were involved? Was it predominantly a relationship, task, or process conflict?
2. Identify the role cognitive bias and emotions played in some difficult situations you have encountered in school.
3. How might conflict be harnessed to serve as a tool for school improvement?

NOTES

1. Sharon Salzburg Quotes, no. 76. The original quote may be found in Sharon Salzburg, *Real Love: The Art of Mindful Connection* (New York: Flatiron Books, 2017).

2. Goksoy and Argon, "Conflicts at School and Their Impact on Teachers," *Journal of Education and Training* 4, no. 4 (April 2016): 197.

3. Ghaffar, "Conflict in Schools: Its Causes & Management Strategies," *Journal of Managerial Sciences* 3, no. 2 (July–December, 2009): 212–27, http://www.qurtuba.edu.pk/jms/default_files/JMS/3_2/05_ghaffar.pdf#:~:text=Conflict%20in%20Schools%3A%20Its%20Causes%20%26%20Management%20Strategies,among%20individuals%20and%20groups%20lead%20them%20to%20conflicts.213.

4. Keator, "Dispute or Conflict? The Importance of Knowing the Difference," Mediate, www.mediate.com/articles/KeatorT1.cfm.

5. Hoy and Miskel, *Educational Administration: Theory, Research, and Practice*, 9th ed. (New York: McGraw-Hill, 2013), 17–23.

6. Thien and Razak, "A Proposed Framework of School Organization from Open System and Multilevel Organization Theories," *World Applied Sciences Journal* 20, no. 6 (2012): 889–99, doi:10.5829/idosi.wasj.2012.20.06.2016.

7. Meckler and Rabinowitz, "The Changing Face of School Integration," *Washington Post*, September 12, 2019, table 1, www.washingtonpost.com/education/2019/09/12/more-students-are-going-school-with-children-different-races-schools-big-cities-remain-deeply-segregated/.

8. Wells, Fox, and Cordova-Cobo, *How Racially Diverse Schools and Classrooms Can Benefit All Students* (Century Foundation, 2016), https://tcf.org/content/report/how-racially-diverse-schools-and-classrooms-can-benefit-all-students/?session=1.

9. For further discussion of this topic, see Mujic, "Education Reform and the Failure to Fix Inequality in America," *Atlantic*, October 29, 2015, www.theatlantic.com/education/archive/2015/10/education-solving-inequality/412729/; and Solly, "158 Resources to Understand Racism in America," *Smithsonian Magazine*, www

.smithsonianmag.com/history/158-resources-understanding-systemic-racism-amer
ica-180975029/.

10. Diamond and Lewis, *Despite the Best Intentions: How Racial Inequality Thrives in Good Schools* (Oxford: Oxford University Press, 2015); Patrick, Socol, and Morgan, *Inequities in Advanced Coursework: What's Driving Them and What Leaders Can Do* (Education Trust, 2020), https://edtrustmain.s3.us-east-2 .amazonaws.com/wp-content/uploads/2014/09/08183916/Inequities-in-Advanced -Coursework-Whats-Driving-Them-and-What-Leaders-Can-Do-January-2019.pdf.4.

11. Howard, "As Diversity Grows, So Must We," *Educational Leadership*, March 16–22.

12. Ryan, *Leading Diverse Schools* (New York: Kluwer Academic Publishers, 2003), 8.

13. Northeast and Islands Regional Educational Laboratory, *The Diversity Kit: An Introductory Resource for Social Change in Education* (Providence, RI: LAB at Brown University, 2002), www.brown.edu/academics/education-alliance/sites/ brown.edu.academics.education-alliance/files/publications/diversitykit.pdf.63.

14. Cherry, "How Does Implicit Bias Influence Behavior?" Verywellmind, September 18, 2020, www.verywellmind.com/implicit-bias-overview-4178401.

15. Tatum, "Color Blind or Color Conscious?" School Superintendents Association, www.aasa.org/SchoolAdministratorArticle.aspx?id=14892.

16. Martin, "That's 'The Way We Do Things Around Here,'" *Electronic Journal of Academic and Special Librarianship* 7, no. 1 (2006), https://southernlibrarianship. icaap.org/content/v07n01/martin_m01.htm.

17. Coburn, "Shaping Teacher Sensemaking: School Leaders and the Enactment of Reading Policy," *Educational Policy* 19, no. 3 (July 2005): 476–509, doi:10.1177/0895904805276143.

18. Rosenholz, *Teachers' Workplace: The Social Organization of Schools* (New York: Longman, 1989).

19. Rosenholz, *Teachers' Workplace.*

20. Tyack and Tobin, "The 'Grammar' of Schooling: Why Has It Been So Hard to Change?" *American Educational Research Journal* 31, no. 3 (Fall 1994): 453–79.

21. Albright, Clement, and Holmes, "School Change and the Challenge of Presentism," *Leading & Management* 18, no. 1 (January 2012): 78–90.

22. Kowalski, *The School Superintendent: Theory, Practice, and Cases*, 3rd ed. (Los Angeles: Sage Publications, 2013), 98.

23. Liggett, "Toward a Conceptualization of Democratic Leadership in a Professional Context," *Canadian Journal of Educational Administration and Policy* 193 (2020): 119–25.

24. Uline, Tschannen-Moran, and Perez, "Constructive Conflict," *Teachers College Record* 105, no. 5 (June 2003): 789.

25. Isabu, "Causes and Management of School-Related Conflict," *African Educational Research Journal* 5, no. 2 (May 2017): 148, https://files.eric.ed.gov/fulltext/ EJ1214170.pdf.

26. Heller, "What We Know (and Think We Know) About the Learning Brain," *Phi Delta Kappan* (December/January 2018–2019), https://kappanonline.org/learning -brain-neuroscience-tokuhama-espinosa-heller/.

27. Chick, "What Are Learning Styles?" Vanderbilt University Center for Teaching, https://cft.vanderbilt.edu/guides-sub-pages/learning-styles-preferences/.

28. Kaplan and Owings, *Introduction to the Principalship* (New York: Routledge, 2015), 14–16.

29. Burns and Purcell, "A Formative Assessment Compromise to the Grading Debate," *ASCD Express* 14, no. 31 (July 11, 2019), www.ascd.org/ascd-express/vol14/num31/a-formative-assessment-compromise-to-the-grading-debate.aspx.

30. Kaplan and Owings, *Introduction to the Principalship*, 41.

31. Kaplan and Owings, *Introduction to the Principalship*, 44–47.

32. Kaplan and Owings, *Introduction to the Principalship*, 7–12.

33. Spillane, Reiser, and Reimer, "Policy Implementation and Cognition: Reframing and Refocusing Implementation Research," *Review of Educational Research* 72, no. 3 (September 2002): 387–431, doi:10.3102/00346543072003387.

34. Ghaffar, "Conflict in Schools," 214–15.

35. Ghaffar, "Conflict in Schools," 215.

36. Spillane, Reiser, and Reimer, "Policy Implementation and Cognition."

37. Coburn, "Shaping Teacher Sensemaking."

38. Ramsey, *How to Say the Right Thing Every Time: Communicating Well with Students, Staff, Parents, and the Public*, 2nd ed. (Thousand Oaks, CA: Corwin, 2009), 3.

39. Ramsey, *How to Say the Right Thing Every Time*, 11.

40. University College London, "Energy Demands Limit Our Brains' Information Processing Capacity," ScienceDaily, August 3, 2020, www.sciencedaily.com/releases/2020/08/200803140046.htm.

41. Chai, Hamid, and Abdullah, "Working Memory from the Psychological and Neurosciences Perspectives: A Review," *Frontiers of Psychology* 9, no. 401 (March 27, 2018): 1–16, doi:10.3389/fpsyg.2018.00401.5.

42. Berg, "Leading Together/Retraining the Brain," *Educational Leadership* (May 2020): 86.

43. Finkelstein, Whitehead, and Campbell, *Think Again: Why Good Leaders Make Bad Decisions and How to Keep It From Happening to You* (Boston: Harvard Business Press, 2008), 15–29.

44. Masterclass, "How to Identify Cognitive Bias: 12 Examples of Cognitive Bias," www.masterclass.com/articles/how-to-identify-cognitive-bias.

45. Finkelstein, Whitehead, and Campbell, *Think Again*, 31–53.

46. Finkelstein, Whitehead, and Campbell, *Think Again*, 50–53.

47. Jehn, Greer, Levine, and Szulanski, "The Effects of Conflict Types, Dimensions, and Emergent States on Group Outcomes," *Group Decision and Negotiation* 17, no. 6 (November 2008): 465–95, doi:10.1007/s10726-008-9107-0.

48. Kennedy, "Re: United States Committee for UNICEF July 25, 1963," Papers of John F. Kennedy, Presidential Papers, White House Central Files, Chronological File, Series 1, President's Outgoing Executive Correspondence, Box 11, Folder "July 1963: 16–31," JFKL, www.jfklibrary.org/learn/about-jfk/life-of-john-f-kennedy/john-f-kennedy-quotations.

49. Hill and Tyson, "Parental Involvement in Middle School," *Developmental Psychology* 45, no. 3 (June 2009): 740–63.

50. National PTA, "The Center for Family Engagement," www.pta.org/center-for-family-engagement.

51. Centers for Disease Control and Prevention, *Parent Engagement: Strategies for Involving Parents in School Health* (Atlanta, Georgia: U.S. Department of Health and Human Services, 2012).

52. Fullan, *Change Forces: Probing the Depths of Educational Reform* (London: UKL Falmer Press, 1993), 8.

53. Isabu, "Causes and Management of School-Related Conflict," 149.

54. Crossfield and Bourne, "Management of Interpersonal Conflict between Principals and Teachers in Selected Secondary Schools in Bermuda," *Insights of Anthropology* 2, no. 1 (February 24, 2018): 91.

55. Jehn, "A Qualitative Analysis of Conflict Types and Dimensions in Organizational Groups," *Administrative Science Quarterly* 42, no. 3 (September 1997): 530–57, doi:10.2307/2393737.539–40.

56. Runde and Flanagan, *Developing Conflict Competence: A Hands-on Guide for Leaders, Managers, Facilitators, and Teams* (San Francisco: Jossey-Bass, 2010), 3.

57. Bacal, "Organizational Conflict—The Good, the Bad, and the Ugly," *Journal for Quality and Participation* 27, no. 2 (Summer 2004): 21.

58. Mayer, *The Dynamics of Conflict: A Guide to Engagement and Intervention* (San Francisco: Jossey-Bass, 2012), 35.

59. Goksoy and Argon, "Conflict at Schools," 201.

60. Ghaffar, "Conflict at Schools," 213.

61. Isabu, "Causes and Management of School-Related Conflict," 148.

62. Shoho and Barnett, "The Realities of New Principals: Challenges, Joys, and Sorrows," *Journal of School Leadership* 20, no. 5 (September 2010): 577, doi:10.1177/105268461002000503.

63. Levin, Bradley, and Scott, "Principal Turnover: Insights from Current Principals" (Palo Alto, CA: Learning Policy Institute / Reston, VA: National Association of Secondary School Principals, 2019), para. 11, https:/learningpolicyinstitute.org/product/nassp-principal-turnover-insights-brief.

64. Uline, Tschannen-Moran, and Perez, "Constructive Conflict," 789–92.

65. Jehn, "A Qualitative Analysis."

Chapter Three

Leadership in Conflict

Today, no serious change effort would fail to emphasize the key role of the principal.[1]

—Michael Fullan

You can sense it from the moment you step in the main entrance. There is an atmosphere that permeates a school, aptly called school climate. Some schools exude an airy and welcoming vibe while others feel oppressive and contaminated. Read these actual comments from teachers.

When our school reopened in September with a new principal, the about-face was immediate. Trust was first to go. There was constant turmoil between the principal and staff—everyone from teachers to custodians felt unappreciated. The principal was demanding . . . even rude. Warring factions formed either defending or sabotaging her . . . and faculty meetings became the battlefield. It was a toxic environment. Many of the veterans seemed to withdraw, reciting the mantra "Just close your door and teach." *A lot* of new hires updated their resumes.

For others, the impact of a newly installed principal was inspirational and invigorating.

I've already had more conversations with the principal this fall than the previous four years. You can tell he's going out of his way to get to know us. Having a principal ask what I think is a new experience. He even suggested I join a committee to review the student behavior code. We've been arguing over that issue for ages but nothing ever changes. It's not just me. Even the thirty-year veteran across the hall seems revitalized.

Parents attribute a school's environment, either welcoming them with an open door or erecting barriers, to the building leader. The maxim "Parents-as-partners" may be realized in the form of shared events such as back-to-school night, committees composed of stakeholders writing school policies, parent-teacher and parent-principal conferences evidencing equality of status and voice, and even perhaps a willingness to hear adverse feedback from each other.

Just as often, in conversations around the coffee urn at PTA meetings and in the stands during weekend sports tournaments, parents critique inexplicable delays from school personnel responding to requests for meetings or answering email and voicemail messages and complain of perceived intimidation tactics. Picking up the telephone, the principal is greeted with "I'm calling you because there is no point in talking to that teacher anymore." Barreling into the office, a teacher commands, "I won't meet alone with that parent," demanding back up from the administrator.

Chapter 1 reported a 2019 *Education Week* poll that found 19 percent of teachers deemed parent issues a major source of friction in the teacher-principal relationship.[2] The National Center for Education Statistics 2019 National Household Education Survey discovered only 56 percent of parents were "satisfied with the way school staff interacts" with them.[3] In such an environment, it can be inferred there is considerable discord.

The principal's influence on adult relationships and school climate and culture is well established in school improvement literature and the anecdotal experience of professional, parent, and other community stakeholders. The quality of interactions, the palpable tenor of the school, the way school business is conducted—all these facets of school life are determined, to a great extent, by the building's leadership.

In *Qualities of Effective Principals*, Stronge, Richard, and Catano's extensive literature review affirmed "the effective school leader's role in fostering and sustaining a positive school climate"[4] by "building relationships" and promoting "respect and recognition of staff, parents, and members of the school community,"[5] among other variables. Marzano, Waters, and McNulty's meta-analysis *School Leadership That Works: From Research to Results*, highlighted the impact of a leader imbuing school culture with "shared beliefs and a sense of community and cooperation among staff."[6]

As school leaders have the capacity to transform school culture, so too they shape the way schools manage conflict. Ghaffar notes, "The conflict isn't the problem—it is when conflict is poorly managed that is the problem."[7] Asking staff and parents about the principal's role vis-à-vis conflict prompts a panoply of responses. Quite frequently, it is alleged the principal is the cause of discord or seems powerless to smooth friction between adults in the building.

Runde and Flanagan postulated the concept of "conflict competence" that leaders instill to facilitate productive outcomes.[8] They delineated seven constructive leadership behaviors in conflict situations (see table 3.1).

Table 3.1. Runde and Flanagan's Constructive Leadership Behaviors.

Constructive Leadership Behavior	Description
Perspective taking	Empathy and understanding another person's view.
Creating solutions	Outside-the-box problem-solving ability
Expressing emotions	Calm demeanor builds trust
Reaching out	Willingness to apologize
Reflective thinking	Astute analysis of group interactions
Delaying responding	Taking time-out lowers the emotional temperature
Adapting	Being flexible and optimistic

Source: Craig E. Runde and Tim A. Flanagan, *Becoming a Conflict Competent Leader: How You and Your Organization Can Manage Conflict Effectively* (San Francisco: Jossey-Bass, 2007), 132–64.

Gerzon characterized three distinct types of leaders dubbed demagogues, managers, and mediators and assessed the impact of each one on conflict.[9] The demagogue is associated with historically despicable figures such as Hitler and Stalin, dictators proclaiming themselves and their followers superior human beings and demanding blind obedience. Gerzon found a form of demagogue leadership in everyday organizations both sowing and managing conflict using attack tactics, one of the 3 *A's*.

> On a smaller scale, this kind of bias-based leadership can occur in organizational politics and in ordinary civic life. The lie of a superhuman "we" and a subhuman "they" can emerge in any human system. In organizations, demagogic leadership relies on turning an executive, an employee, or a department into a scapegoat. Demagogues repeatedly resort to blaming someone else for any failures and to achieving success through employees' fear of becoming the next scapegoat.[10]

Managers, according to Gerzon's model, have benign intentions and genuinely offer benefit: organizations need competent managers. The limitation of the manager's conflict style is exclusivity. While they are viewed as supportive and effective leaders within their own clique, a parochial perspective restricts them to single-minded devotion to their own turf while neglecting alternative vantage points and lacking a broad systems approach. Gerzon described the problem with managers' approach to conflict as follows.

The leaders . . . are decent, competent, caring men and women. But they do not
lead effectively in high stakes, multi-sided situations, because they are thinking,
and acting, like managers. They are leading inside a box and being defined by
their turf. If these leaders do not broaden their perspective and take on the role
of leader as mediator, these differences will sooner or later spark conflict that
breeds inefficiency, lowers trust, produces friction, and, if not healed, leads to a
breakdown in the system of which they are a part.[11]

In schools, manager-types may form an informal club of like-minded educators who share the same pedagogical philosophy and even speak the same
education jargon. A single-minded focus on the club causes them to disregard
disagreement, allowing feelings of detractors to fester until, on occasion, loud
protests erupt from disaffected parents or staff. Every few years emergency
meetings might be called to defend a particular approach to teaching reading,
for example.

Under a manager, discord is never resolved, it simply retreats. As Gerzon
observed, the limitations of the manager's style become more pronounced as
issues rise in complexity. Managers are incapable of leading through conflict
if the issue is race or inequality because remediating these concerns requires
absorbing alternative perspectives beyond the horizon of the insular group.
The ideal leader in Gerzon's view is the mediator. Gerzon's characterization
almost waxes poetic.

The Mediator . . . is able to turn conflict into a positive force for achieving a
larger purpose. This kind of leader transforms conflict from a force that can be
destructive and divisive into one that is healing and connecting. Since we human
beings urgently need to make conflict work for us rather than against us, those
who can lead through conflict hold the key.[12]

THE 3 *A'S* APPROACHES TO CONFLICT LEADERSHIP

Chapter 1 introduced three basic responses to conflict, the 3 *A*s: attack,
avoid, and address. To exemplify how each approach might be manifested in
the case of a school implementing an education initiative, imagine a school
leader's attempt to launch project-based learning in every classroom. For
some faculty accustomed to a traditional teacher-directed style, the new peda-
gogy represents a ground-shifting transformation. The learning curve for the
teacher could be steep: guiding students through the inquiry process, cultivating their interests, and overseeing twenty-five individual projects.

Anticipating resistance, a principal in attack mode capitalizes on institutional rewards, threats, and punishments to suppress dissent. Points of
leverage at the principal's disposal include classroom observation ratings,

complimentary or critical; coaching or extracurricular club stipends offered or withdrawn; assignment of desirable or undesirable teaching schedules; assignment of convenient or inconvenient parking spots.

These are not the only types of clout principals exert. Most people prefer to work in an environment where they enjoy their supervisor's positive regard. The principal's smile or friendly tone of voice is in itself a powerful motivator. In the school-wide curriculum development example, an aggressive principal would divide and conquer, keeping uncertain and indifferent teachers and potential opponents off the curriculum planning committee in order to squelch their voices. The leader chooses only allies, derisively dubbed the "principal's pets," or requests volunteers, cunningly realizing only acolytes are likely to enlist.

A principal with a propensity to avoid conflict takes advantage of a phenomenon described in chapter 2: schools are popularly misconstrued to be tightly coupled organizations characterized by centralized command and control when in fact most schools are decentralized, loosely structured systems.[13] "Just close your door and teach" is a widely repeated refrain among colleagues recognizing the realpolitik of a teacher's capacity to act independently.

In the project-based learning curriculum adoption illustration, a conflict-averse principal allows unlimited discretion, resulting in wide variation from one classroom to the next. Some teachers might implement a student-centered model in which each student decides on a research topic ranging from Arthur the Aardvark to organic zucchini while other teachers, spurning individualization, prescribe a specific subject.

The principal might shun classroom visits in order to avoid observing inconsistent practices and standards and therefore dodge any reason to intervene. An avoidance strategy, "administrative orbiting," is the practice of attesting that "everything is always 'under consideration'—let's study, document, then cancel meetings."[14] Many educators are familiar with committees that meet endlessly without reaching an outcome or peter out after a few sessions.

To management experts speaking on the McKinsey Podcast, a variation of conflict avoidance is facile agreement, defined as a propensity in a meeting to render "low commitment decision(s)."[15] Out of an exaggerated sense of politeness, "we all shake our heads and nod 'yes' in the room. And then we leave" and the decision is reversed. Or "they give a very soft disagreement. But it's so soft that you can choose to ignore it, and so people with a hidden agenda do."[16]

The time-honored strategy of picking the low-hanging fruit has merit in certain circumstances. It's a good place to start while the organization is first developing conflict-agility. The problem occurs when organization members never reach for higher branches. Then singular attention to a school's least-challenging difficulties becomes the go-to avoidance strategy.

Diamond and Lewis relied on extensive observation, interviews, and questionnaires to examine racial inequity in a diverse suburban high school in *Despite the Best Intentions: How Racial Inequality Thrives in Good Schools*.[17] The authors unearthed, for example, a pattern of black teenagers facing harsher discipline consequences, and a disproportionate percentage of white students enrolled in advanced placement courses. The authors attributed these practices to America's racist legacy and systemic factors such as poverty at home and parents' educational attainment.

They found, however, that behavior and beliefs among staff, students, and parents of the high school were also determinative. For instance, responding to parental pressure, teachers and administrators regularly granted white students admission into accelerated classes although they did not meet the entrance criteria. While the school's written policies were race neutral and individual staff adjudicating policies were not considered racist, data clearly demonstrated the presence of a racial hierarchy. As the title of the book avows, *despite the best intentions*.

But why didn't anyone do anything about it? From interviews, the authors quote high school students, parents, teachers and administrators who were aware of the injustices. The causes of inaction should not be oversimplified. There were deeply planted historical, political, economic, educational, and sociological roots. But one of the reasons was the unwillingness of school leaders to confront the issue, hoping to avoid the dissension that would inevitably surface.

Enforcing advanced placement admission criteria consistently no doubt would provoke friction between white parents who know how to manipulate the system and school staff. Despite universal agreement the existing condition is inequitable and unfair, altering the status quo would be extremely destabilizing, requiring leaders from the high school, central office, and board of education to deal with conflict.

Appeasement is another form of avoidance. Masquerading as problem solvers, school leaders may offer ready agreement in order to forestall conflict. Like other forms of avoidance, though, the problem with appeasement is its failure to fully process dispute, a shortcut that causes conflict to fester.

Between the category of attack and avoid is passive aggressiveness, defined by the American Psychological Association Dictionary as "behavior that is seemingly innocuous, accidental, or neutral but that indirectly displays an unconscious aggressive motive."[18] Passive aggressive principals give disfavored staff the cold shoulder or direct the secretary to defer a meeting with a teacher questioning an evaluation report. Parents are motioned to sit in juvenile furniture while the teacher literally looks down from an adult desk chair. While tacit, the effect of these behaviors is to assert a power advantage and thus they are characteristic of an attack.

The leader addressing conflict, the third *A*, involves diverse voices on an ongoing basis. In one of our schools where project-based learning was implemented, the staff had practiced group problem solving during regular faculty meetings the previous three years and therefore were prepared to work out differences in the planning phase. A curriculum planning committee, representative of the faculty in its membership, surveyed teachers to be responsive to their concerns. After the program launch, they met for two more years to make modifications on the basis of ongoing staff feedback.

Conflict-agility refers to productive conflict resolution skills. Developing these skills is akin to toning muscles. Muscles strengthen with exercise; similarly, the school community becomes increasingly adept the more conflict-agility skills are practiced and as a healthy conflict mindset becomes integrated into the culture. At our schools, conflict-agility language ("That's interesting. Tell me more" or "This is where we agree. These are the issues we need to work out") began to proliferate in parent conferences and staff meetings. Establishing cultural norms is the ultimate destination; the starting point is building trust.

BUILDING TRUST

On the basis of experience, members of organizations large and small understand that trust is the foundation of effective leadership. "Trustworthy leadership is at the heart of successful schools," writes Tschannen-Moran in a book aptly titled *Trust Matters: Leadership for Successful Schools*.[19] Lencioni's *The Five Dysfunctions of a Team: A Leadership Fable* posits five maladaptive group dynamics beginning with the most basic: absence of trust. He asserts, "Trust lies at the heart of a functioning, cohesive team. Without it, teamwork is all but impossible."[20]

What is trust and how is it grown? Lencioni defines trust as "the confidence among team members that their peers' intentions are good and that there is no reason to be protective or careful around them."[21] He offers telltale indicators of a dearth of trust including a reluctance to ask for help, hiding mistakes, making snap judgments about others, and holding grudges. Sound familiar?

When we are confronted with an incompatible view, the tendency is to presume others are acting out of less-than-pure motives and flawed competence. (The corollary is that one's own motives and competence are unassailable.) It is not sufficient to simply disagree, the character of the other person must be disparaged too. "There the parent goes making excuses for the child." "The teacher doesn't care about kids."

There is a host of problems caused by the tendency to impugn motivation. It exacerbates differences and is never productive. Assumptions are made about the interior of someone's heart. Immediate issues—the child's behavior under discussion in a parent conference, the merits of a curriculum initiative—are deflected. Drago-Severson and Blum-DeStefano note, "In our teaching and research, *trust* [emphasis added], safety and respect have emerged as vital *preconditions* for supporting growth."[22] They relate these necessities to Maslow's hierarchy of needs: an organization's aspirational objectives cannot be met without a foundation of trust, safety, and respect.

The relationship between trust and conflict-agility is equivalent to the chicken-or-the-egg question. On one hand, trust is a prerequisite to the development of conflict-agility in an organization. On the other hand, as Tschannen-Moran states, "cultivating more productive ways of dealing with conflict is an important part of building a culture of trust in schools."[23] It's impossible to say which comes first; trust and conflict-agility grow and diminish in tandem. What is clear, however, is that trust helps prevent task and process conflicts from degenerating into relationship conflicts that can have an enduring impact on group cohesiveness.[24]

In addition to trust-boosting behaviors, there are also trust-busters, the latter category including broken promises, follow-through failures, and criticism behind someone's back. Lencioni suggests a number of exercises designed to engender trust, some very familiar.[25] For example, group members may share results of their Myers-Briggs personality inventory, leading to a better understanding of why they disagree as in "You're an intuitive-feeling-type and I'm a sensing-perceiver." Be with a faculty long enough and one conference day you'll find yourself staring up at a ropes course intended to instill faculty cooperation.

Below you'll find key strategies and guiding principles you can employ to promote conflict-agility. As noted in chapter 1, each strategy will be indicated by a pushpin icon.

📌 *Be a Role Model*—Building trust begins with the leader personifying a model for organization members to follow by nurturing an emotionally safe, nondefensive space for free exploration of ideas. In order to hear an alternative point of view, the leader must first reject proprietary ownership of all the right answers. Other qualities associated with trustworthy leadership are honesty, reliability, and competence. (It's hard to establish trust if the school is in disarray.)[26] To Fullan, enhancing trust is a function of "relationships, relationships, relationships."[27]

❦ *Honor Errors*—Engendering trust necessitates a positive outlook regarding mistakes committed by organization members: errors are inevitable and even useful because they offer a powerful learning opportunity. Lencioni highlights the benefits of a leader modeling personal vulnerability, a necessary prerequisite to "create an environment that does not punish vulnerability."[28]

If teachers feel they'll be reprimanded for missteps, their inclination is to obscure them, ultimately nullifying the opportunity to fix the problem on a systemic scale. Castigating errors has the effect of discouraging risk-taking and initiative from which improvement springs. No less a creative thinker than Albert Einstein, asked to share his life's motto, is purported to have replied, "A person who never made a mistake never tried anything new."

❦ *Don't Play the Blame Game*—When a school's shortcomings are mentioned in a grade-level, department, or faculty meeting, the next order of business often is to hunt for someone to blame or to seek absolution. Countless principals in the era of No Child Left Behind, after opening staff meetings with the observation "Our standardized test scores have dropped," have been greeted with remarks attributing fault such as "The class came with a reputation from last year" or "Did you ask the remedial reading teacher?"

Similar to censuring mistakes, blaming interferes with the development of trust, diverts productive problem solving, and exhausts energy. An effective speech in response to fault-finding is "I wasn't looking for someone to blame. Let's figure out how we can find a remedy together." Perhaps no leadership proclamation is more welcome than a well-timed "I have your back."

❦ *Break with the Past*—Reflecting on the past is fraught territory since people enter conversations and relationships hefting emotional baggage from earlier perceived slights. When revisiting emotionally charged past events is unavoidable, the leader's role is to ensure history is not allowed to undermine the future. By saying "We'll look backward for a few minutes but mostly we'll look ahead," the leader gives permission to rehash bygones with the understanding that the ultimate goal is to move forward.

❦ *Set Parameters*—A frequent complaint heard among planning committee members is "There was no use serving on the committee. The principal had already decided." Often the accusation holds an element of fact: the leader may be insistent on pre-established, non-negotiable ideas. When these expectations are hidden, trust is eroded and not just among the present committee; since institutions have long memories, future committee work is jeopardized as well. That's why a leader must disclose parameters from the beginning.

WHAT'S GOING ON?
UNDERSTANDING CONFLICT IN YOUR SCHOOL

Leaders perceive the organization in their charge through a lens. One of the challenges they face is to put aside their emotions and prejudices to see through another lens. Heifetz and Linsky describe this practice in *Leadership on the Line: Staying Alive Through the Dangers of Leading.*[29] A central metaphor in the book is the image of a dispassionate leader observing the organization from the distance of a balcony in order to take stock of the behavior of the members below.

If you're standing on a crowded ballroom floor, you may have the impression that everyone is dancing, but from the perspective of the second tier, it becomes evident that the number of dancers rises and falls with the tempo. The balcony analogy is similar to an anthropological orientation that enables a cultural observer to hold in abeyance pre-formed beliefs. (This topic is discussed further in chapter 4.)

The following are some caveats to consider whether you're standing on Heifetz and Linsky's balcony or looking through an anthropologist's multifocal lens.

 The Issue Isn't the Issue—Without judging or choosing sides, what is really going on? In one of our first principalships, Seth was mentored by an assistant superintendent who often sagely commented, "The issue isn't the issue," meaning there may be unexpressed, perhaps even subconscious, underlying issues. For example,

- a parent might vociferously complain about a school's excessive homework policy causing nightly tear-filled episodes when the real concern is the child struggling with an executive function disability in combination with an overwhelmed adult attempting to juggle work and home responsibilities.
- a teacher's perceived knee-jerk opposition to a curriculum initiative might reflect uncertainty over managing yet another innovation crammed into the finite hours of a school day.

The process of examining the layers beneath superficial language is frequently called peeling back the onion. It is the leader's job to help identify what the speaker is really trying to say.

 There Is Always a Kernel of Truth—A superintendent colleague frequently suggested to the administrative team, "Even when you disagree, there is always a kernel of truth." Chapter 2 explored the influence of cognitive bias in exacerbating conflict. One example predisposes people to accept a "belief that judgments that differ from one's own are either uninformed, a product of intellectual incapacity or laziness, or a reflection of distorting motivational, ideological, or cognitive bias."[30] Another fallacy is in-group bias, which attributes sole legitimacy to the beliefs of an insular clique. When group members are predisposed to reject alternative perspectives, it's the leader's job to say, "Maybe they have a point."

❧ *Seek First to Understand*—Stephen Covey, author of *The 7 Habits of Highly Effective People*, coined the adage "Seek first to understand."[31] Try the following exercise. During the next conference you attend, mark an *X* on scrap paper every time someone asks a question. There's a good chance the paper will still be blank when the conference ends. Of the three typical punctuation marks that can end a sentence (periods, exclamation points, and question marks), the last one is undoubtedly least common in adult conversation.

Leaders can structure a protocol to encourage active listening and dispel the tendency for meeting participants to reflexively assert their opinion in response. Before information is conveyed, the leader might announce, "After the presentation, I'd like you to reserve judgment for ten minutes. We'll discuss the idea, and ask clarifying questions. There will be time to critique later. First, let's understand with an open mind." Alternatively the leader might state, "I'll reiterate what you said. Let me know if there's anything I missed or did not fully appreciate" or might invite participants to restate each other's views.

❧ *Defend Against Defensiveness*—A defensive response invariably results in an us-versus-them and win/lose dynamic. "I'm under attack, therefore you and I are opponents, and only one of us can be right." The other deleterious consequence of defensiveness is that behind a defensive wall, the listener often misses the intended meaning of the message. Runde and Flanagan suggest two remedial steps: "cooling down" (being aware of the potential to become angry), and "slowing down" (taking a step back to view the big picture).[32]

Fullan maintains leaders require emotional intelligence since "in a culture of change, emotions frequently run high."[33] Adapting Goleman's conception, Fullan delineates two broad categories of emotional intelligence: personal and social competence. Leaders demonstrating personal competence are self-aware and able to self-regulate their emotions; socially competent leaders are adept in social situations, motivate others, and instill empathy.[34]

Say a parent calls to complain about a disciplinary consequence or a teacher denounces a year-end performance evaluation. Instead of responding instantly with a justification, first breathe deeply, recognize there may be underlying concerns, and say, "That's interesting. Tell me more." Suppose a combative meeting between union representatives and the administrative team is anticipated. Require each party to remain silent for ten minutes while they listen to the other then restrict follow-up to clarifying questions that deepen understanding, bridge the us-versus-them divide, and nurture trust as group members realize their voices will be heard.

CREATING A MINDSET: CONFLICT WITHOUT DISSENSION

A leader's words and actions determine whether conflict is perceived as a natural and potentially productive byproduct of change or as threatening and harmful. In the name of avoiding hurt feelings or in a desire not to roil smooth seas, many leaders assume conflict necessarily sparks divisiveness. Or does it? Is it possible for staff to disagree among themselves, or to differ with parents, without debilitating discord?

Fullan describes the transformational power of conflict in which "dissent is seen as a potential source of new ideas and breakthroughs. The absence of conflict can be a sign of decay."[35] The premise is for adults to understand that conflict, respectfully communicated, will not cause personal pain and permanent rifts. Tschannen-Moran expresses the point with an eye on national headlines: "In a fractured society characterized by increasingly discordant public discourse and diminishing civility, trustworthy school leaders stand for something different. They let constituencies know that conflict and distrust are not necessarily the last word."[36]

To the extent the principal can imbue a school with the notion that disagreement is a natural and ultimately productive part of the group problem-solving process, then conflict becomes an accepted even a positive characteristic defining the school community. Diverse opinions and the working out of differences emerge as valued facets of a group's identity. The objective is to contextualize conflict in a positive narrative.

🏵 *First Things First*—Leaders often exhibit the tendency to advance their own agenda first. Conflict-agility encourages leaders to understand that organization members are unlikely to accept an administrator's policy or program objectives until their own concerns are addressed. When being introduced to an inquiry learning initiative, for example, teachers may need to resolve concerns about the impact on their schedule before they can fully consider the curriculum change.

🏵 *Center Conversation Around Ideas, Not People*—The way to avoid personalizing conflict is to shift conversation to the arena of concepts where philosophical differences can be discussed dispassionately with less risk of breaching trust. One way to accomplish this is to be quick to respond when disagreements become increasingly personal; instead, refocus attention on the demands of the task or the specifics of the process needed for implementation of change.[37]

Additionally, school leaders can follow Zwilling's advice on "curious confrontation," which he defines as "simply facing differing ideas with the desire to investigate and learn."[38] The emphasis is on ideas; specifically, a conversation in which participants open an inquiry to explore each other's viewpoint. Effective leadership language promotes a focus on ideas. For example, "That's an interesting idea. Please say more about it" implies a thought has validity and merits further discussion while "Let's talk about what the issue is . . . and what the issue is not" opens the door to clarifying that a disagreement is not personal or threatening.

Sometimes finding something positive to say to wrap up a contentious meeting requires a lot of searching. A recommendation, if there is no consensus yet to be found, is to applaud good intentions. For example, "I know that we all have the best interests of our students at heart even if we can't agree on the details so far."

🕭 *Emphasize Agreement*—A conflict-agility mindset requires confidence in a positive outcome. By highlighting the group's progress and emphasizing areas of agreement, there is acknowledgement that the task of reaching consensus is underway. Another strategy to build confidence in ongoing discussions is to note that disagreement is, in the popular phrase, no big deal. In the heat of dispute, a leader may remind a group that the perception an issue is contentious or weighty often becomes exaggerated. Many once-impenetrable historical impasses have been peacefully resolved; most school controversies are not insurmountable.

🕭 *You're Doing What You're Supposed to Be Doing*—Everyone has roles to play in an organization, and often their interests are at odds. In these cases it is important to accord respect, normalize dispute, and remind everyone that relationships will remain amicable. A phrase that can be employed in such circumstances is "You're doing what you should be doing, advocating for your child (or representing your colleagues)." It's a way to express "We may disagree, but I understand you."

🕭 *There Are Words to Respectfully Deliver Any Message*—Tschannen-Moran conceives of school leaders as coaches.[39] Imagine a parent calling a principal to complain about a teacher. Specifics might entail a grade, homework, or the child's comfort in class. Often the principal's ultimate goal is to open direct lines of communication between the parent and teacher. To get there, the parent might be nervous about approaching the teacher. The principal may coach the parent on how to convey the message in a manner the teacher will hear.

Principals frequently lie awake at night wondering how they can inform a teacher of a decline in an annual performance rating without causing irreparable damage to their working relationship. These situations summon another truism: There is a way to respectfully deliver any message. The principal's role is to find the words for a productive conversation with the teacher or to coach the parent before the parent-teacher conference.

ESTABLISHING SCHOOL CULTURE: MAKING CHANGE LAST

In *Leading Change Together*, Drago-Severson and Blum-DeStefano suggest that "culture sits at the heart of individual and systems change" before going on to say that "cultivating a positive culture is one key responsibility of educational leaders."[40] Fullan makes the leader's role in promoting cultural change even more pronounced: "Transforming the culture—changing the way we do things around here—is the main point . . . Effective leaders know the hard work of reculturing is the sine qua non of progress."[41]

Cultural shifts take time. Past experiences establish expectations, social dynamics, and patterns of behavior that leaders may naively underestimate. When we started conflict-agility practices in our schools, the first stabs were lonely and feeble. After a time, our conflict-agility skills and the acceptability of these practices grew. We began to notice teachers and other school leaders were employing the language of conflict remediation with each other and then with parents. "That's interesting." "I'd like to repeat what I hear you saying to see if I have it right."

Conflict-tolerant terminology that began in an administrator's office was eventually repeated in faculty, grade-level, department, leadership, and parent meetings. This was gratifying and also a crucial development because it was an indication that conflict-agility was becoming integral to school culture. Like any cultural practice, it is self-reinforcing. As more school community members adopt a new orientation, they become agents of fundamental change.

⚡ *A "For the Good of the Community" Protocol*—A protocol for use at the beginning of faculty meetings, which we call "For the Good of the Community," enables a school to address immediate issues while toning the school's conflict-agility muscles. A detailed description of the protocol is provided in table 3.2. Common practice when organizational problems are raised is to blame and accuse. Both the cause of the trouble and the responsibility to fix it invariably rest with someone else. The stipulation that "everyone agrees to be part of the solution" reorients responsibility from individuals to the community.

For example, in Seth's school, a teacher stood before the faculty one April day to report a rash of "spring has sprung" behavior in the middle school hallways. In prior days, the teacher might strike an accusatory tone, suggesting administrators were unaccountably absent. Applying the For the Good

Table 3.2. For the Good of the Community Protocol

Before *For the Good of the Community*	*During* *For the Good of the Community*	*After* *For the Good of the Community*
1. To avoid surprises, send an email requesting agenda items 2–3 days in advance. If a submission does not meet the criterion (see below) or if there is insufficient time available, have a one-on-one conversation before the meeting. 2. Agenda items must pertain to most of the faculty. No pet peeves or parochial grade or department issues.	1. Before the teacher presents the issue, remind the faculty of the ground rules: • No blaming or finger pointing. • Everyone must be part of the solution. 2. Discussion lasts no more than ten minutes at the beginning of the meeting.	1. While wrapping up, review the quality of group interactions, focusing on the process. 2. After ten minutes if the issue is not resolved, appoint a committee to report back at the next faculty meeting or sooner via email. More extensive issues can be directed to a broad-based team (see chapters 4–6).

of the Community process, teachers and school leadership together explored various causes and possible remedies and developed a plan.

Previously, teachers detecting problems like "spring has sprung" were more likely to keep it to themselves or grouse when they gathered with colleagues, lacking a productive forum where they might raise the issue and devise a remedy. In time, the most significant outcome of For the Good of the Community was a cultural shift toward acceptance of shared responsibility for problem solving.

🍓 *Pick the Low-Hanging Fruit*—The low-hanging fruit analogy represents solving the simplest, most straightforward problems first. After a few successes, group problem-solving skills improve, trust and confidence in the process grow, and a new culture begins to take shape. As organization members increasingly perceive themselves capable of working together and solving disagreement without animosity, conflict is no longer regarded as an impediment.

A word of caution: while picking the low-hanging fruit is an acceptable way to practice problem solving while the group gains skill and confidence, as noted earlier, if the group never advances to thornier issues located on the higher branches of complexity, attending only to low-hanging fruit becomes a form of avoidance. In cases like these, the school's efforts to advance equity begin and end with an annual assembly or a dedicated bulletin board.

🍓 *Create Opportunities for Group Decision Making*—Practices require repetition to become assimilated into organizational culture. In schools, shared decision-making committees, curriculum planning committees, new staff hiring committees, policy development committees, and conference-day planning committees all provide opportunities to reinforce group values, attitudes, and behaviors concerning conflict and collaboration. Runde and Flanagan assert that if teams "want to keep conflicts from derailing their efforts, an essential first step is . . . to establish norms and processes for dealing with the inevitable conflicts they will face."[42]

🜊 *Build Communities*—The more faculty and parents view themselves as a community, the more they will buy into the notion of shared destiny that is essential for group problem solving. Food has a remarkable potential to bring people together: pot luck dinners for parents, get-togethers for community causes, even a staff end-of-year party will all build cohesion and mutual trust. Bit by bit, the us-versus-them mindset fades.

Conflict-agility starts with the leader. The practical strategies suggested in this chapter begin with steps a leader can take to establish trusting relationships. The chapter ends with a focus on how leaders can embed conflict-agility practices in school culture, making collaborative ownership of problem solving part of "the way we do things around here."[43] That's emblematic of effective leadership, beginning with individuals while ultimately molding the cultural gestalt.

CHAPTER SUMMARY

In the annals of school improvement literature, the principal's influence cannot be understated. As a role model, the principal exemplifies the school's modus operandi and ultimately imbues the school culture with a perspective on conflict. This chapter identified three leadership approaches to conflict: *attack* the opposition by meting out threats, punishments, and rewards; *avoid* discord by neglecting, minimizing, or endlessly studying controversial issues; and skillfully *address* conflict, recognizing its productive potential.

The leadership techniques suggested in the chapter included trust-building strategies leaders may enact and trust-busters to eschew; exercises to guide leaders in better understanding organizational conflict and engage the school community in conflict without dissension; and a blueprint to acculturate a healthy approach to conflict, consequently increasing the school's capacity for change.

CONTEMPLATING CONFLICT

Here are some questions for your consideration as you think about the contents of this chapter.

1. Reflect on a leader who influenced you as a positive role model or a negative exemplar you would want to avoid. In relation to conflict, what was each leader's typical style? How do you believe the leader's approach to conflict affected the school?
2. In each of the sections of chapter 3, select one promising practice you can implement tomorrow.
3. You've been tasked to plan a conference for teachers in your school that applies the lessons of this chapter to parent-teacher conferences. What are some key points you will convey to help teachers lead more productive conferences?

NOTES

1. Fullan, *The New Meaning of Educational Change* (New York: Teachers College Press, 2016), 124.

2. *Education Week*, "Principals, Here's How Teachers View You," October 16, 2019, www.edweek.org/leadership/principals-heres-how-teachers-view-you.

3. National Center for Education Statistics, *National Household Education Survey* (Washington, DC: U.S. Department of Education, 2019), 15.

4. Stronge, Richard, and Catano, *Qualities of Effective Principals* (Alexandria, VA: Association for Supervision and Curriculum Development, 2008), 17.

5. Stronge, Richard, and Catano, *Qualities of Effective Principals*, 25.

6. Marzano, Waters, and McNulty, *School Leadership That Works: From Research to Results* (Alexandria, VA: Association for Supervision and Curriculum Development, 2005), 48.

7. Ghaffar, "Conflict in Schools," *Journal of Managerial Sciences* 3, no. 2 (July–December, 2009): 213, www.qurtuba.edu.pk/jms/default_files/JMS/3_2/05_ghaffar.pdf#:~:text=Conflict%20in%20Schools%3A%20Its%20Causes%20%26%20Management%20Strategies,among%20individuals%20and%20groups%20lead%20them%20to%20conflicts.

8. Runde and Flanagan, *Becoming a Conflict-Competent Leader: How You and Your Organization Can Manage Conflict Effectively* (San Francisco: Jossey-Bass, 2007).

9. Gerzon, *Leading through Conflict* (Boston: Harvard Business School Press, 2006).

10. Gerzon, *Leading through Conflict*, 20.

11. Gerzon, *Leading through Conflict*, 33.

12. Gerzon, *Leading through Conflict*, 50.

13. Kowalski, *The School Superintendent*, 3rd ed. (Los Angeles: Sage Publications, 2013), 98; Weick, "Educational Organizations as Loosely Coupled Systems," *Administrative Science Quarterly* 21, no. 1 (March 1976): 1–19.

14. Bacal, "Organizational Conflict—The Good, the Bad and the Ugly," *Journal for Quality and Participation* 27, no. 2 (Summer 2004): 21.

15. De Smit, London, and Weiss, "To Unlock Better Decision Making, Plan Better Meetings," McKinsey Podcast, November 9, 2020, www.mckinsey.com/business-functions/organization/our-insights/to-unlock-better-decision-making-plan-better-meetings#.

16. De Smit, London, and Weiss, "To Unlock Better Decision Making."

17. Diamond and Lewis, *Despite the Best Intentions* (Oxford: Oxford University Press, 2015).

18. VandenBos, *American Psychological Association Dictionary of Psychology*, 2nd ed. (Washington, DC: American Psychological Association, 2015), 767.

19. Tschannen-Moran, *Trust Matters: Leadership for Successful Schools* (Hoboken, NJ: Wiley Publishing, 2014), 268.

20. Lencioni, *The Five Dysfunctions of a Team* (San Francisco: Jossey-Bass, 2002), 195.

21. Lencioni, *The Five Dysfunctions of a Team*, 195.

22. Drago-Severson and Blum-DeStefano, *Leading Change Together: Developing Educator Capacity within Schools and Systems* (Alexandria, Virginia: Association for Supervision and Curriculum Development, 2018), 50.

23. Tschannen-Moran, *Trust Matters*, 263.

24. Jehn, Greer, Levine, and Szulanski, "The Effects of Conflict Types, Dimensions, and Emergent States on Group Outcomes," *Group Decision and Negotiation* 17, no. 6 (November 2008): 470, doi:10.1007/s10726-008-9107-0.

25. Lencioni, *The Five Dysfunctions of a Team*, 197–201.

26. Stronge, Richard, and Catano, *Qualities of Effective Principals*, 20–22.

27. Fullan, *Leading in a Culture of Change* (San Francisco: Jossey-Bass, 2007), 51.

28. Lencioni, *The Five Dysfunctions of a Team*, 201.

29. Heifetz and Linsky, *Leadership on the Line: Staying Alive through the Dangers of Change* (Boston: Harvard Business Review Press, 2002), 51–74.

30. Ehrlinger, Readinger, and Kim, "Decision-Making and Cognitive Biases" *Encyclopedia of Mental Health*, 15, www.researchgate.net/publication/301662722_Decision-Making_and_Cognitive_Biases/link/59d7ee80a6fdcc2aad0650e7/download.

31. Covey, *The 7 Habits of Highly Effective People: Personal Workbook* (New York: Simon & Schuster, 1989).

32. Runde and Flanagan, *Becoming a Conflict-Competent Leader*.

33. Fullan, *Leading in a Culture of Change*, 74.

34. Fullan, *Leading in a Culture of Change*, 72.

35. Fullan, *Leading in a Culture of Change*, 74.

36. Tischanen-Moran, *Trust Matters*, 263.

37. For further information, see the discussion of Jehn's work in chapter 2 of this book.

38. Zwilling, Martin, "Ten Top Attributes Elevate Design Thinking Leaders," AlleyWatch, December 6, 2017, www.alleywatch.com/2017/12/10-top-attributes-elevate-design-thinking-leaders/.

39. Tschannen-Moran, *Trust Matters*, 258–61.

40. Drago-Severson and Blum-DeStefano, *Leading Change Together*, 45.

41. Fullan, *Leading in a Culture of Change*, 44.

42. Runde and Flanagan, "How Teams Can Capitalize on Conflict," 21.

43. Martin, "That's 'The Way We Do Things Around Here,'" *Electronic Journal of Academic and Special Librarianship* 7, no. 1 (2006).

Chapter Four

Building Understanding

The best way to have a good idea is to have lots of ideas.[1]

—Linus Pauling

Chapters 1 through 3 discussed sources of conflict in schools as well as the vital role played by principals and other school leaders in developing a culture and climate conducive to the productive resolution of conflict. This chapter shifts attention to design thinking, a process for addressing wide-ranging, deep-seated issues that result in conflict while simultaneously strengthening the conflict-agility a school needs to meet long-term challenges.

Design thinking evolved in earnest during the last half of the twentieth century when attention turned to the solution of "wicked problems," that is, complex situations that appear to be poorly defined, include seemingly contradictory elements, and require multilevel responses. Wicked problems resist traditional approaches to generating solutions. They require collaborative, creative responses that are rooted in the needs of end users. Early adopters of design thinking came from the disciplines of engineering and architecture. However, the past few decades have seen the expansion of the approach into many other fields.[2]

Design thinking is structured for addressing difficult, multilayered problems. At its heart, design thinking is a people-centered process that recognizes the importance of incorporating diverse perspectives in decision making as well as respecting the emotions of those involved—considerations that schools must take into account in order to implement changes that last.

Design thinking enables stakeholders to develop perspectives that encompass both the dance floor and the balcony, a metaphor used with great effectiveness by Heifetz and Linsky.[3] The collaborative work embodied in

design thinking builds bridges across interpersonal, demographic, ideological, political, and organizational boundaries[4] and is a valuable asset for open
systems like schools that include multiple stakeholders and must maintain
complicated—and often problematic—relationships with the environment.

Design thinking's methods prompt intense levels of creative thought. The
model views obstacles as opportunities for novel solutions. The approach
goes beyond out-of-the box thinking, instead encouraging participants to
abandon self-imposed constraints on problem solving by thinking "without
the box."[5]

With a wide-angle lens, design thinking takes a holistic approach to
change, recognizing that many of the problematic situations encountered in
schools are not clearly defined at first glance and typically involve the interplay of many factors and actors.[6] At the same time, however, design thinking
requires participants to zoom in on the specific context at hand, an orientation that is particularly relevant for institutions like schools that are deeply
influenced by—and irrevocably connected to—the unique histories, cultures,
composition, and practices of their communities.

Two of design thinking's stages—prototyping and testing—help schools
avoid the paralysis-by-analysis syndrome that often plagues decision making.
The rigor of design thinking also builds problem-solving skills among collaborators, thereby promoting a sense of collective efficacy, a shared belief in
a group's ability to work together to achieve meaningful goals.[7]

STAGES OF DESIGN THINKING

Tim Brown, former CEO of the renowned consulting and design firm IDEO,
frames design thinking as a process involving three components: inspiration,
ideation, and implementation. Inspiration represents the issue that requires
problem solving. It can begin with a "wonder question" to prompt collaborative work.[8] Ideation refers to the process of generating possible pathways to
address the problem.[9] Implementation occurs as potential solutions are applied to the situation at hand, with the best solution selected as the ultimate
response.

The Hasso Plattner Institute of Design at Stanford (often referred to as the
"d.school") offers a widely known model of design thinking that expands on
Brown's framework. Its version serves as the one that organizes this book's
remaining chapters. The d.school framework conceptualizes the process as
composed of five steps: empathize, define, ideate, prototype, and test.

The d.school model, like others related to the field, emphasizes that design
thinking entails collaborative effort rather than solitary work. Collaborators

in design thinking are provided with license to generate creative ideas, add insights to each other's viewpoints, and provide each other with feedback that helps refine initially fuzzy notions into actionable proposals. Design thinking provides a safe arena that promotes involvement across organizational and social boundaries and thereby allows conflict to be aired, examined from multiple perspectives, and addressed with innovative solutions that address dissension's roots.

Empathize, the first stage of the model, identifies the parties most affected by the problem (the "users" in design thinking lingo) in order to understand their perspectives, priorities, needs, and interests. Much like ethnographic studies, the empathize stage directs problem solvers to develop a "thick description"[10] of the lived experience of stakeholders that recognizes their beliefs *and* feelings in order to ensure the relevance and applicability of the work to come.

Actions taken to develop empathy align with what conflict expert Mark Gerzon calls "integral vision," that is, the development of a full appreciation of the positions taken by actors in a conflict.[11] In schools, the empathy stage must always incorporate an understanding of student needs.

The next stage, define, provides an opportunity for the group to share the findings gathered in the empathize stage and make certain that the key actors in the dispute have been identified. Once this has been accomplished, design thinkers (called "designers" or "design team members" from this point forward) need to ascertain the various perspectives on the issue, define outcomes that will remedy the discord by addressing the needs of those involved, and anticipate how those now in conflict will think and feel when the issue in contention is resolved.

Work in define consists primarily of problem finding rather than problem solving.[12] In this regard, it is also critical to remember the dictum that "the issue is not always the issue." Defining requires deep reflection and often results in the realization that what appears to be a personality conflict is at its base a larger organizational issue centered on task and process. Defining enables designers to develop "systems thinking,"[13] an appreciation of the way in which the various aspects of a conflict influence each other.

When designers ideate, they take initial steps toward finding a solution. The ideate stage recalls the original use of the term "think tank" in World War II as a safe space where ideas could be generated and discussed. The vision in the ideate phase is expansive. It operates in the realm of possibilities rather than practicalities, rejecting the inclination to say "Yes, but" by replacing it with "Yes, and."[14] Fluency is the goal in this phase. In the non-judgmental ideate environment, multiple potential solutions to a crisis emerge that move beyond tried-and-true, hackneyed answers.

Whereas ideating demands divergent thinking, a nonlinear process, prototyping requires its opposite: convergent thinking. Implementation begins in the prototype stage. Participants in the prototype stage create theories of action, a set of "If . . . then . . ." statements that describe how a proposal will be enacted and what results are anticipated to follow. One might view the results of prototyping as a kind of colander through which only the ideas most fitted to the existing situation flow.

Testing is the final component of the design process. Feedback is collected at this point to determine whether the solution meets the needs of those involved. If those needs have not been fulfilled, the process typically returns to ideate for further analysis and improvement.

The components presented above provide a concise summary of the five design thinking elements. The remainder of this chapter explores the first three elements (empathize, define, ideate) in depth while chapter 5 will address the remaining two (prototype and test).

Before moving forward, however, a qualification is needed: although this division of labor describes the model, it also makes it appear that the design thinking process is always sequential, with one stage serving as the prerequisite for the next. In actuality, the process is iterative. Designers may find themselves still working to increase levels of empathy even as their preliminary understandings lead them to begin the process of ideation. Similarly, feedback from stakeholders in the latter stages of the process may make it clear that the designers have missed the mark, taking them back to previous empathy, define, or ideate efforts.

Consider this illustration of the iterative process in action. A school experiencing rapid demographic change might stage a multicultural fair proposed by the design team as a way to ease tensions among members of the school community and promote mutual understanding only to find that some stakeholders view the effort as tokenism and therefore refuse to participate. Such a circumstance would necessitate a return to ideate to develop other possible solutions. The flexibility of design thinking's stages is a strength as it provides designers with opportunities to refine their ideas with increasing levels of precision.

ESTABLISHING THE FOUNDATION

While design thinking can be a potent force for addressing conflict, it cannot simply be injected into the structures of a school. Successful implementation requires a foundation built on a set of leadership understandings and practices.

Like a good novel, design thinking requires principals and other school leaders to suspend disbelief and invest in the possibility that something seemingly far out of reach can in fact become reality. The process also requires time and collective effort, resources that are often at a premium in schools. Without an appreciation of the obstacles that may be encountered on the road to addressing conflict through design thinking, principals may be sidetracked into unproductive detours or abandon the route before the impact of the process can be realized.

As a first step, school leaders must keep in mind the role that emotion plays in their own decision making. Leaders are expected to be rational, to be able to put their emotions aside and employ logic to generate ideas and take action. In fact, the image of leaders calmly evaluating the merits of alternatives defies reality. The brain always operates with both reason and emotion; the two cannot be separated.

Chip and Dan Heath refer to this duality as the dynamic of the elephant and the rider.[15] The elephant represents the emotional self while the rider symbolizes rationality. The relative size of the elephant when compared to the rider shows how easy it is for logic to be derailed and feelings to dominate.

All problematic situations automatically arouse the emotional side of the brain. This can be particularly significant for school leaders, who deeply feel the weight of their responsibility to students and the school community at large. While such feelings can raise needed caution flags in some situations, they can also arouse fears about taking the wrong steps and thereby inhibit action.

Conflict increases the level of challenge even further. Pressure to restore tranquility, coupled with perceptions of threat, can enable the feelings-based elephant to overwhelm the logic-based rider.[16] Rationality suffers, replaced at least temporarily by a fight-or-flight stance (the *A*s of *attack* and *avoid*) that erects barriers to communication and understanding.

Emotionally charged situations can also induce the use of cognitive bias to create a sense of order and speed decision making. As discussed in chapters 2 and 3, these mental-shortcut biases include fundamental attribution error, which ascribes behavior to personal characteristics rather than situational factors; confirmation bias, which interprets events in a manner that supports one's own views; and in-group bias, which is a tendency to support those belonging to one's own social group rather than outsiders. The last category is particularly important as leaders seek to tackle school issues intertwined with broader concerns about privilege and equity.

Leadership consultant Michael Hyatt adds another perspective on how the imperfect processes of our own thinking can lead us to make bad decisions. He identifies three "decision-making traps" that can limit our willingness to recognize the drivers of difficult situations and encumber our search for remedies.[17]

The first trap, "the Rosy Scenario," reflects confirmation bias. In this case, leaders shape all information into positive projections that support their own views. In schools, this tendency may lead principals to ignore a brewing conflict over a new curriculum initiative by viewing discontent merely as growing pains.

The second trap, "the Wrong Ingredient," results in a rush to judgment that misidentifies the factors leading to success. Here principals may mistakenly attribute improvements in reading scores to test preparation rather than the impact of classroom instruction.

Hyatt's final trap, "Binary Thinking," limits the quest to find alternatives to a given problem to a choice between two extremes. Binary thinking may lead a principal to frame a conflict over discipline policy as a choice between an orderly school and one in constant chaos.

Knowing the cognitive and emotional tripwires that can ambush sound decision making in conflict situations is one thing; avoiding them is another. How can principals and other school leaders develop and maintain the strong degree of self-awareness and self-control needed to use the design thinking model most effectively?

Identifying the issues or behaviors that trigger strong personal reactions is vital. To accomplish this difficult task, Runde and Flanagan identify two steps. The first, "slowing down," provides time to consider not just one's own thoughts but the emotions, ideas, and concerns of the others caught in a challenging moment. Slowing down provides time for cooling down, that is, lowering the emotional temperature that constrains sharp thinking.[18]

Principals interested in addressing conflict through design thinking must also ground their efforts in a growth mindset. They must recognize that all members of the school community, not just children, possess a shared human potential for developing character, talent, and particularly creativity,[19] and they must consistently demonstrate confidence in that ability to promote personal growth.

On a broader scale, design teams must work within a supportive organizational culture.[20] Principals must take the lead to ensure that "the way we do things around here" includes values, norms, and practices that sustain a deep commitment to solving wicked problems and facilitate robust dialogue and collaboration. Trust serves as a foundational element of this commitment. School leaders must also remember their impact as role models and exemplify through their actions that they walk the talk.

In addition to trust, design thinking requires a commitment to collaboration that extends beyond formal job titles and listens to a wide array of voices.

Leadership actions that value the contributions of each stakeholder (and during the design process, of each team member) and celebrate teamwork demonstrate such a commitment. In the same fashion, it is important to encourage all participants to respectfully challenge the views of others regardless of their position in the organizational chart, a process that the creative dynamo Pixar refers to as creating a "challenge network."[21]

School culture should also promote the collective efficacy of faculty by recognizing accomplishments and valuing collaborative work. Collective efficacy can be viewed as shared, affirming belief in agency, a feeling that translates to the expression "We've got this." Research demonstrates that a sense of efficacy can sustain group effort.

Principals and other school leaders can foster a belief in collective efficacy by highlighting gains that have been achieved, providing opportunities for teachers to conduct action research on problems of practice, offering professional development to increase team-building skills, and celebrating success. Collective efficacy is a powerful force. Once firmly established, it becomes self-reinforcing, producing even greater commitment to group effort.[22]

Somewhat paradoxically, at the same time that design thinking thrives in a culture of collective efficacy, it also requires an acceptance of risk taking and the associated understanding that mistakes are likely to be made. Participants need license to venture from the well-beaten path in gathering information, to develop and advocate for novel alternatives, and most importantly, to learn from missteps along the way.

IDEO's Tim Brown summarizes this aspect of the process with the advice "Fail early to succeed sooner."[23] Typically such flexibility is rare in schools, which are often constrained by chains of command, regulations, demands by policymakers for accountability, and deeply held beliefs about structures and practices conceptualized as "the grammar of schooling."[24]

Similarly, the non-linear nature of design thinking mandates patience and a tolerance for ambiguity. The process as it unfolds can appear muddled and uncertain. Designers may move back and forth between stages several times before advancing a preferred solution. The iterative process for the refinement of ideas occurs at a fast pace, but allowing thoughts to develop fully cannot occur in a culture that demands quick, carefully sequenced solutions. Research on team development suggests that teams take time to mature into high-functioning groups, a progression Tuckman conceptualizes as "form, *storm*, norm, and perform."[25]

Design thinking embraces a diversity of viewpoints and encourages participants to challenge prevailing beliefs that wicked problems cannot be solved. To ensure that all aspects of an issue are considered, particularly those related to resolving inequity, schools implementing design thinking must commit themselves to seeking contributions from all members of the school community including those traditionally marginalized in educational matters who may be reluctant to share their thoughts with those perceived to be indifferent or even hostile to their ideas and feelings.

Just like school leaders, designers must be aware of the potential for overt and hidden bias to influence conclusions. They must hold their emotions in check as they consider positions that may differ markedly from their own. They must control tendencies to preemptively dismiss as inaccurate the stories others tell of their experiences in school. Instead, they must accept the stories as valid representations of the way others interpret aspects of school life and they must use them in the solution process even if it creates a level of discomfort.

LAUNCHING DESIGN THINKING

Design thinking's practices can be used to address issues that are limited in scope or affect broad swaths of the school community. In the business world, a design thinking project typically begins with a design brief. The brief might include the context of the market issue or engineering task to be addressed, agreed-upon benchmarks to use in assessment, a timeline, and a budget.

Schools operate in different environments, of course, but the brief still holds value. It can be used as a starting point, a figurative anchor when a design team needs to be convened to address a wide-ranging, complex issue that affects a significant segment of the school community and will take a fair amount of time to resolve.

In such contexts, the design brief should include a concise description of the situation at hand, the anticipated outcome of the work of the group, a rough timeline, any resources that will be provided or made available, and the method by which the team will communicate its findings, conclusions, and recommendations (e.g., a report, a presentation, a model). Because schools do not operate in a vacuum, the brief should also identify any constraints (laws, regulations, budgetary limitations, etc.) of which the design team must be aware.

School leaders should be mindful that many school initiatives fail because participants do not understand the scope of the work, receive vague or conflicting directions on how to proceed, propose solutions that violate accepted policies or practices, or wander so far afield that their final proposals have little connection to the initial charge. An organizing structure and clear goal statement therefore increase the likelihood of success. While some design team members may bristle at any limitations on the group's prerogatives, long-term benefits will accrue when briefs offer boundaries to keep activities relevant and focused.

Developing a design brief requires a touch of artistry. As the launching point for the process, it must promote sustained participation by engaging hearts and minds (the elephant and the rider) in an intense focus on understanding the conflict, a phenomenon Mark Gerzon calls "presence."[26] Principals also need to balance the brief's focus on structuring the design experience with the need to encourage creativity and risk taking.

The brief cannot be received by the school community as merely one of many memos issued by the principal's office, and the design team itself cannot be discounted as "just another committee." Studies of workplace motivation conducted by the consulting firm McKinsey and Company offer guidance on how to inspire engagement among members of a design team.

McKinsey suggests connecting the task at hand to sources of meaning: benefitting society; helping the organization achieve optimal performance; providing superior service; enjoying positive team experiences; or reaching personal goals for growth.[27] McKinsey's recommendations may be supplemented with Gerzon's advice to focus on relationships rather than abstractions as well as the Heath brothers' conclusion that both sound ideas *and* passion are needed to facilitate change.[28]

If a full design team is needed, how many members should it have? Team composition in schools can be dictated by contract, past practice, budget, school culture, and, of course, political considerations. In general, however, smaller is better. Smaller groups provide more opportunity for teammates to communicate clearly and develop strong connections with each other. They also diminish the potential for a phenomenon known as "social loafing" in which team members assume that others will pick up the slack as their own efforts decrease.

The size of a design team depends on other factors too. Some issues will require technical expertise, perhaps a wizard with achievement data analysis, a specialist with a deep understanding of disabilities, or someone fluent in a language spoken by many members of the school community. Strong digital skills might be valuable as well. Diversity in terms of gender, ethnicity, age, and experience in schools can be helpful in creating stimulating discussions, ensuring relevance and cultural competence, and arousing creative juices.

One special social skill also stands out: the ability to connect with those outside one's circle.[29] Team members with this aptitude are invaluable assets in the design process as they can readily engage the broader community, keep everyone apprised of progress, and offer insightful feedback and direction as the group works through the various design stages.

Now consider the following case as the basis for developing a brief for a full design team.

Whonabee Elementary School, a K–5 school with deep roots in its community, is experiencing a wave of debate about homework policy. The squabbling started when a parent at a PTA meeting called for making permanent the school's pandemic-based commitment to "no homework except reading for pleasure." Although no decision was reached at the meeting, word of the parent's statement spread quickly through the school community.

Three camps emerged, each with very strong opinions about what should be done. One group ardently endorsed the parent's demand, sharing research that suggested homework has little value for younger students and emphasizing the need for time for play and socialization. A second group supported the school's existing policy of ten minutes per day in kindergarten and grade one with ten additional minutes for each succeeding grade, noting that the policy had served the school well for a long time. A third group insisted on a new policy that would substantially raise the homework expectations for grades four and five, a change advocated as a way to promote higher levels of achievement in reading and mathematics as well as prepare students for the rigors of middle school.

Interestingly, each perspective was supported by a cross-section of the school community; one could find parents and staff advocating for any of the positions. Board of education policy allowed each school much leeway in connection with homework. For all intents and purposes, Whonabee was on its own.

Noah Storrie, the principal of Whonabee, was amazed by the speed with which the conflict took hold among stakeholders as well as the divisive ripples it created in other aspects of school life. Distance seemed to take the place of collegiality, tension gripped PTA events, and gossip about which position the school administration secretly favored became the norm. Principal Storrie decided it was time to convene a design team to address the homework dispute.

Table 4.1 presents the design brief to set the stage for the project. It leads directly to initiation of the design process.

ACTIVATING EMPATHY: THE FIRST STAGE

Although design thinking is an iterative process, its foundation in any given circumstance always rests on empathy with those identified as users. In a school, users are those stakeholders in the school community who are most directly impacted by the dissonance that spawned the conflict. Note that this category may include members who are not actively involved in the dispute at the moment as there may be individuals and groups that have a significant interest in the topic but for one reason or another have not taken a role in the debate.

Table 4.1. Homework Policy Design Brief

Problem	The school's homework policy is the subject of widespread debate among school community members. The conflict distracts us from our mission and divides us into factions. Most importantly, it leads us to question how we approach our work with our students. To provide the best possible instruction for students and heal our school community, we need to determine the role of homework in Whonabee's program in terms of developmental appropriateness and value.
Anticipated Outcome	Identification of specific modifications (if any) of current policy, accompanied by their rationale *or* Identification of the rationale for maintaining the current policy
Design Team Membership	Four representatives of the faculty with a diversity of years of experience and teaching assignments; four members selected by PTA representing the diversity of the membership; one representative from school leadership
Timeline	October through February
Communication of Findings	Presentation at faculty meeting Presentation at PTA town hall convened for this purpose
Process	Design thinking stages of empathize, define, ideate, prototype, test
Resources	Access to aggregate school student achievement data; polling and survey apps; team meeting room; supplies and materials needed for group meetings and storage of data and documents; clerical support as needed; limited release time for staff members (subject to approval of principal); dedicated school email and Zoom accounts for design team members; refreshments for meetings; limited budget for other incidentals
Constraints	Cannot contradict board policy; must respect student and family right to privacy; must respect union contract; cannot exceed budget; should assume current curricula remain in place; cannot address staff evaluation.

The category should always include students. Even if not involved directly, students must be considered users at some level as everything in schools should ultimately be connected to addressing their needs.

The goal of the empathize stage is to leave one's own conceptions, perceptions, and feelings behind in order to develop an informed, comprehensive understanding of what the parties in the conflict think and feel. As we might define "empathy" to a student, we seek to put ourselves in other people's shoes.

The task could seem simple enough: gather a lot of information. However, holding one's own perspectives and biases in abeyance is always challenging. It requires the skill of an investigative reporter, the sensitivity of a clinician, the doggedness of a detective, and the insights of an anthropologist. To the greatest extent possible, designers at this stage need to become experts about the trees *and* the forest—that is, the details of experience deemed important by disputants as well as the patterns that connect them.

Ethnographers sometimes characterize their role as what John Van Maanen called "making the familiar strange rather than the strange familiar."[30] The wordplay crisply captures the strategy by which an investigator creates thick descriptions of life not as an outsider looking in but as an insider looking out. Designers in the empathize phase begin their work with a commitment to "look, listen, and learn."[31]

Conn and McLean advocate that problem solvers approach situations with a "dragonfly eye." Dragonflies, they note, possess large, compound eyes that enable them to take a 360-degree view of the environment. They explain the value of the metaphor by adding, "Think of this as widening the aperture on a problem or viewing it through multiple lenses. The object is to see beyond the familiar tropes into which our pattern-recognizing brains want to assemble perceptions."[32]

Of course, humans could never approach the visual powers of a dragonfly just as dragonflies will never identify the complex interplay of factors that make up human behavior. People, however, can become highly competent sleuths capable of keen observation and eliciting the perceptions, observations, and opinions of others. Conn and McLean emphasize that data gathering should focus on "occurrent behavior," that is, observed action in context, an antidote for the tendency to rely upon previous, possible, or projected behavior.[33]

Specifically, designers should take careful note of what people say and do in connection with the conflict to be addressed, considering them "look fors" and "listen fors" just as they would in a classroom observation. In this quest, it is important to attend to both figure and ground. Table 4.2 provides examples in each category.

Simply observing, however, is not enough. To gain a full understanding of conflict situations, one also has to engage more directly with the participants. Just as in the classroom, questioning can be an invaluable tool in this regard. Conn and McLean extol the value of asking why as in "Why is this so?"[34]

❧ Digging deeper, designers might ask,

- What exactly is the problem that needs to be solved?
- What is most important to you about this situation right now?

Table 4.2. Look Fors and Listen Fors in Empathy Observations: Figure and Ground

Figure	Ground
What comments are made about the topic?	What are the patterns? Where are they made? When are they made?
Which aspects affect the experience of students?	How does this issue relate to the mission and vision of the school?
Who makes the comments?	To what groups do these participants belong? (Consider all possible memberships including demographics; position in the school; team, grade-level, and content area specialties; relationship to the students; role in the community; family arrangements; etc.)
Who are the primary actors? Supporters? Observers?	
How do those holding different views interact?	What are the social relationships among them? What are the power relationships among them?
What are the specific circumstances in which the conflict is observed?	What patterns (time, place, participants) emerge from these observations? When is the conflict accelerated or decelerated?
What are the words, actions, or situations that are most emphasized?	What type of conflict does this seem to be? Task? Process? Relationship? What value-laden words provide clues about the perspectives of participants?
What emotions are observed? When are emotions highest? Who exhibits the strongest emotional involvement in the conflict?	What are the pain points? How might these reflect deeply held values? Does the emotional temperature change depending on who is present or participating?
What non-verbal communication is observed?	What does non-verbal communication reveal about different aspects of the conflict? What does non-verbal communication reveal about the depth of the disagreement?
What data, artifacts, and other information sources are associated with the conflict? (Examples include memos, data, and records relating to school activities)	What is the importance of data, artifacts, and other information in creating and sustaining the conflict and informing the search for solutions?
What organizational structures are involved? (Examples include decision-making processes, schedules, and communications methods)	How do organizational issues create, sustain, or extend the conflict?
What social media trail exists?	How does the content of social media illuminate the conflict? How does it sustain or extend the conflict?
What do people say about previous attempts to address the conflict?	What insights can be developed by looking at these failed attempts?
Who is performing at a high level despite the conflict?	What's working? What strategies for success can be gleaned from the approaches these people take?

- How do you see this issue?
- How would you explain this conflict to someone unfamiliar with our school?
- How would you explain it to your colleagues (or families and friends)?
- What frustrates you about the current status of ____?
- How did we get here?
- What's been tried or not tried?
- What have we been missing?
- What needs to change in order to resolve this?
- What is something we could do right now to address this?
- What's standing in our way?
- If only we could . . . then . . .

To encourage sustained, frank conversation, designers must listen without judgment and demonstrate respect both verbally and non-verbally. Empathy can be communicated by expressions of interest and concern for the views of others. While it may be necessary to ask clarifying questions, it's important to talk less in order to learn more. Checking for understanding is also useful to ensure that the speaker's intent has been accurately captured. In this regard it is best to use the speaker's actual words rather than paraphrasing.

Designers should also pay attention to the stories participants tell about a conflict. Storytelling exists in every culture. It provides the means by which complicated and complex events, understandings, perceptions, and emotions can be woven into a cohesive whole. Laura Osburn, a research scientist at the University of Washington, succinctly captures the value of stories by declaring, "We tell ourselves and others stories about who we are, what we do, and why we do it."[35] Stories told about a conflict provide a window into the lived experience of those involved and identify the critical elements that keep the fires of discord burning.

Design team members should record their findings on a timely basis to avoid as much as possible having the information influenced by their own emotions or hidden biases or lost due to the limitations of memory. The notes should capture the salient details of the interaction with quotes used whenever possible. As a summative exercise, designers might create empathy maps: graphic, easy-to-understand representations of their findings and conclusions. Figure 4.1 presents a template for an empathy map that could be adapted for use in Whonabee Elementary School's homework policy project.

Empathy maps may also be created digitally by the design team like those presented in figures 4.2 and 4.3 using the Padlet app.

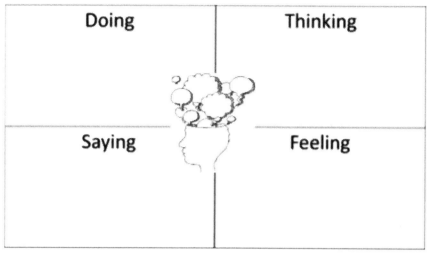

Figure 4.1. Empathy Map Template

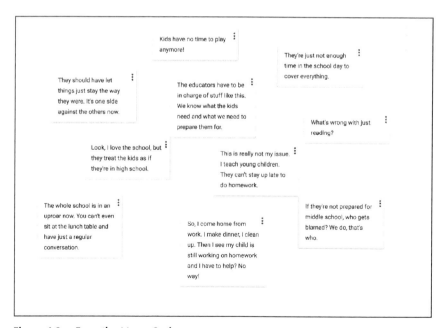

Figure 4.2. Empathy Map—Saying

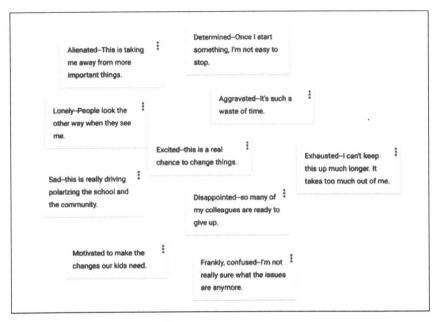

Figure 4.3.   Empathy Map—Feeling

DEFINE: WHAT IS THE PROBLEM OR OPPORTUNITY?

The empathy map serves as a springboard to the next stage of design thinking: define. The goal in this stage is to establish a clear, agreed-upon statement of the problem to be addressed—an accomplishment that will focus group attention on the most critical aspects of the issue. In this phase, the design team must perform two actions often represented in common metaphors: the team must determine the scope of the problem creating the conflict (going beyond the proverbial tip of the iceberg); and they must dig deep into the debate to determine the core of the issue (as in peeling an onion).

The define stage requires pooling the information and insights gathered by the designers as part of the figure-and-ground exercise. As in the empathize phase, guiding questions can help focus attention on the most salient aspects of the conflict. Some of these questions might cause discomfort but they must be addressed in order to develop an accurate representation.

⚓ Examples of guiding questions include

• Which members of the school community are most actively involved? How do they regard the issue?

- Who is indirectly involved but nevertheless must be taken into account? How do they regard the issue?
- How will this promote student learning and growth?
- Based on the observations, what assumptions and values energize, catalyze, or sustain the discord?
- How do social groups and alliances affect the situation?
- What are the hopes and fears of the participants?
- What are the task elements of the dispute? The process elements? The relationship elements?
- What do the data say?
- What is the history?
- What organizational structures, policies, or practices are involved?
- Who (if anyone) is being supported by the situation? Who is being exposed? How so?
- What are the ripple effects in the school community?
- Most importantly, what is the story this conflict tells?

With the information on the table, the design team can build a coherent picture of the multi-sided forces affecting the situation as well as the problem most central to the conflict. To reach this end with accuracy, the team must make sure that the information now at hand aligns with the problem presented in the design brief and points the design team toward an achievable, if challenging, target that will guide the solution process. The result serves as a kind of mission statement for the ensuing stages of the process. Like a good news article, the define statement should identify who, what, why, and (sometimes) where (not necessarily in that order).[36]

Three caveats should be kept in mind as work proceeds on the define statement. First, the statement should focus on the people involved in the conflict rather than technical aspects of the dispute. Second, the statement must be narrow enough in scope to address the specific situation encountered in the school directly rather than broad goals like "ensuring equity" or "changing how schools are funded." Keeping eyes centered on the local issue will increase the likelihood of maintaining group focus over time. Third, the statement should not be so constrictive that it stifles the creative thinking needed to address the wicked problem causing the conflict.[37]

For Whonabee, the define statement might read,

A conflict about homework has engaged our community in divisive debate. It reflects deeply held differences in values and understandings about learning and child development. We will respectfully address these differences and develop a policy recommendation that identifies the *purpose* and *form* of homework for students in our school, expressed in clear, non-technical terms, accompanied by a rationale in support of this stand. The recommendation will help our students use their time outside class in ways that best promote long-term academic and social-emotional growth.

If the team experiences difficulty constructing its definition of the problem, creative juices might be stirred by encouraging members to think in the positive, with the problem turned on its head to be seen not as a threatening crisis but rather as an opportunity for school improvement.[38] Imagery in this context may have more impact than words. The Heath brothers advocate the use of a "destination postcard," a graphic depiction of what things will be like once the conflict has been addressed.[39] Once the picture has been completed, an opportunity statement caption can be developed to accompany it.

DISCOVER POSSIBILITIES: IDEATE

As noted earlier in this chapter, the goal of the ideate component is to identify creative pathways for remedying the conflict. When teams ideate, they consider the world of possibilities and "think without the box."[40] Introducing criteria for the evaluation of proposals at this stage would drastically inhibit creativity and prematurely close off avenues that might prove productive. Divergent thinking is required: team members want to expand the universe of solutions rather than rule any out.

Thinking in this fashion can be challenging. Problem solving in conflict situations is usually associated with a sense of urgency that advocates for rapid responses rather than more time-intensive exploration of the world of possibilities. Quick, well-defined solutions also enable our logical brains to channel emotions to the pursuit of an identified goal. Ideation, on the other hand, is inherently messy, like the pieces of an unsolved puzzle when one first opens the box.

To help designers feel comfortable in what can be a novel situation, a half-dozen ground rules must be observed.

1. Respect each other.
2. Defer judgment.
3. Focus on the core issue not symptoms.
4. Encourage originality.
5. Accept ambiguity.
6. Build on each other's contributions.

When groups get together in a school setting to generate new ideas about a particular set of circumstances, they often begin by brainstorming. The technique can produce good results but it also has limitations that may inhibit creativity and invention.

Typically brainstorming protocols require individuals to share their ideas in a round-robin or similar arrangement. Practices of this kind can discourage contributions that stray far from the conventional, resulting in groupthink that sacrifices innovation as a result of perceived peer pressure. Additionally, the more reticent group members may yield the floor to more boisterous or assertive colleagues. The brisk pace of brainstorming in its traditional format may also hamper the quest for novel ideas as it limits the time for reflection (this aspect may be particularly problematic in virtual meetings). Even so, numerous alternatives exist.

✣ *Brainwriting* begins with individual contemplation. Participants respond to an issue by writing down their own responses. Once the allotted think time ends, each team member shares their ideas with another team member who then is charged with adding an enhancement or a related idea. The process continues as one member shares with another until either all participants have seen all contributions or a facilitator calls a halt to the activity. A master list is then created for further group discussion.

✣ The goal of *mindmapping* is to create a graphic representation of how a potential solution connects with the manifestations of the conflict observed or identified in other stages of the design process. Mindmaps are constructed to make relationships readily apparent to the viewer, and they can be utilized as either an individual or group activity. Figure 4.4 presents a basic template.

✣ Imagery takes the center stage with *picture possibilities* in which designers create pictures that represent proposed solutions. At early stages of the design process and before ideas are refined, thinking in terms of images can stimulate thinking and unleash the imagination. Artistic expertise is not required; in fact, elaborate drawings may obscure proposed solutions by

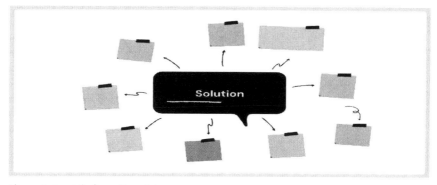

Figure 4.4. Mindmap Template

diverting attention needlessly to scrutiny of details. Team members can also use images from online sources, photographs, or abstract designs as long as they can explain the significance of the selections. Images can be shared among the group and then modified to refine ideas.

    ✤ *Worst idea* takes into account the tendency to find it easier to think negatively rather than positively.[41] In this exercise, designers present tongue-in-cheek alternatives that raise, rather than lower, the level of conflict by offering what they consider to be horrible, counter-productive ideas. The process can revitalize ideation by producing a radical change in perspective while also injecting a note of levity into very intense discussions. After some dreadful ideas have been shared, attention can be turned to identifying strategies diametrically opposed to them.

    ✤ Potential solutions for task conflicts also may be elicited through use of the SCAMPER technique. This acronym stands for substitute, combine, adapt, modify, put to another use, eliminate, and rearrange.[42] Each component is driven by specific questions (see examples in table 4.3). Participants use the categories as discussion starters but it is not necessary to address each section.

    ✤ The last suggestion to promote ideation is perhaps the simplest: *wish*. To use this technique, designers begin with a blank slate, clearing their minds of any assumptions about what is possible or not possible. In wish mode, nothing is out of reach. The laws of nature, entrenched patterns of behavior, time constraints, or caps on resources do not apply. After providing time for each designer to develop a wish list, team members share their thoughts and then work together to identify the thoughts most interesting and relevant to the problem at hand.

    In the next phase, the group takes the ideas that survived the first cut and considers how elements of these far-fetched notions might actually be brought to fruition. Critical questions at this point include

- Why is this an attractive idea? How can we move this from hopes and dreams to reality? Where could we start?
- What assumptions are holding us back from making this happen?
- How strong are the barriers that mitigate against this solution? How can they be overcome?
- If someone who didn't know the situation looked at this idea, what would they suggest to achieve it?

As a final note on ideate, be aware that ideation can be demanding but it also can be very invigorating. Indeed, some design teams may find it so cap-

Table 4.3. SCAMPER Model Questions

SCAMPER Component	Sample Questions
Substitute	• What can be substituted for what we are currently doing without jeopardizing our school's mission and goals? • What other resources can be used to achieve the desired impact? • Where else can this take place?
Combine	• Are there things that can be made simpler? • How can we get individuals or groups to work together to promote synergy, efficiency, and collaboration? • How can we do this while doing something else?
Adapt	• How can we make things more flexible? • How can technology help us? • What are we currently doing that could be adapted to help address this issue? • What have we done before that might be useful in this situation?
Modify	• What can we do to speed up or slow down to help this situation? • What do we need more or less of to address the issue? • What needs to be added to something we already do to improve things? • How can we work smarter not harder?
Put to another use	• Can what we do now be used in some other way? • Who might be better equipped to address this issue? • Is this resource (materials, staffing, technology, time, etc.) being used optimally? If not, how can that use be improved?
Eliminate	• How can we achieve our goals without this? • What would happen if we didn't have this? • How can we streamline things? • What rules or practices are no longer needed? • What wouldn't be missed if we changed things?
Rearrange	• What would happen if we reversed the process? • How can we rearrange the current situation for better results? • What if we consider it backward? • Can we interchange or exchange one thing for another? • Is there a better sequence for this? • Do we all have to start in the same place? • What can be reorganized to produce better results for the students? • How can we change the pattern of behavior?

tivating that they get stuck at this point, stay in the ideate mode too long, and lose the momentum needed to forge ahead in the design process.

Schools have a long history of talking about problems in great depth but failing to implement solutions. Principals must be sensitive to this possibility. If it becomes apparent that the group feels satisfied with just generating ideas and seems hesitant to determine their actual impact on the conflict at hand, designers need to be nudged into the remaining steps: prototype and test (see chapter 5).

Before moving ahead, however, it is again important to recall that the design process does not always proceed in a linear fashion. Even in the prototype and test phases, designers may find it necessary to revisit empathy, define, or ideate to ensure that they capture the core of the issue creating the conflict and advance potential solutions that focus on people's needs, values, and interests.

CHAPTER SUMMARY

Design thinking offers great potential for tackling wicked problems that cause conflict in schools—the ones that have many layers, involve many players, and seem resistant to solution. Design thinking rests upon a foundation of collaboration and respect for the diverse ideas and feelings of others. Creativity is celebrated, and participants in the problem-solving process, the design team, are encouraged to think without the box.

Design thinking blends structure with flexibility. A well-known model for the process consists of five stages: empathize, define, ideate, prototype, and test. This chapter focuses on the first three stages by suggesting that engagement in the empathize, define, and ideate stages can remove the blinders that mask opportunities for improvement and collaboration and spark invigorating feelings of joy, empowerment, and possibility.

The goal in the empathize phase is to understand the views, feelings, and needs of those involved in conflict. In define, those involved in the solution process seek to identify the heart of the issue and an outcome that may resolve it. The ideate stage begins the search for specific solutions with participants encouraged to develop an abundance of creative approaches to the identified issue. While these (and the remaining two) components follow each other in logical order, the process is iterative in nature: in practice, participants may go back and forth between stages as they work to refine understandings and develop the best solutions to vexing challenges.

Design thinking thrives in settings where there are high levels of trust, organizational culture promotes a sense of collective efficacy, and leaders grant design team members permission to fail as they strive to develop the best possible solutions for the issues at hand. This chapter included the foundational elements and practices needed to launch a design thinking initiative in schools and conduct the first three stages.

CONTEMPLATING CONFLICT

Here are some questions for your consideration as you think about the contents of this chapter.

1. Design thinking emphasizes empathy, and this chapter identified several strategies for gathering information about what people are thinking, feeling, saying, and doing. We can observe what people are saying and doing, but since we know that what's unsaid is often at least as important as what's said (or done), how can we best determine what they are thinking and feeling?
2. What is one hot button issue that is currently engaging your school community? Which look fors or listen fors in table 4.2 would seem most useful to help gather information about this issue?
3. What could derail the first three stages of the design process as described in this chapter?
4. What obstacles do you anticipate in bringing design thinking to your school?

NOTES

1. As cited in Olson, *The Art of Creative Thinking* (New York: Barnes & Noble, 1980), 69.
2. Gallagher and Thordason, *Design Thinking for School Leaders: Five Roles and Mindsets That Ignite Positive Change* (Alexandria, Virginia: Association for Supervision and Curriculum Development, 2018), 9–10; Dam and Siang, "Design Thinking: Get a Quick Overview of the History," Interaction Design Foundation, www.interaction-design.org/literature/article/design-thinking-get-a-quick-overview of-the-history.
3. Heifetz and Linsky, *Leadership on the Line* (Boston: Harvard Business Review Press, 2002), 51–74. For additional information, see the discussion of this idea in chapter 3 of this book.
4. Eddington et al., "Addressing Organizational Cultural Conflicts in Engineering with Design Thinking," *Negotiation and Conflict Management Research* 13, no. 3 (August 2020): 264, doi:10.1111/ncmr.12191.
5. Gallagher and Thordason, *Design Thinking for School Leaders*, 54.

6. Khalil and Kier, "Equity-Centered Design Thinking in STEM Instructional Leadership," *Journal of Cases in Educational Leadership* 24, no. 1 (March 2021): 71.

7. Donohoo, Hattie, and Eells, "The Power of Collective Efficacy," *Educational Leadership* (March 2018): 40–44.

8. Gallagher and Thordason, *Design Thinking for School Leaders*, 10.

9. T. Brown, *Change by Design* (New York: HarperCollins, 2009), 16.

10. Geertz, *The Interpretation of Cultures* (New York: Basic Books, 1973), 310–23.

11. Gerzon, *Leadership through Conflict: How Successful Leaders Transform Differences into Opportunity* (Boston: Harvard Business School Press, 2006), 7.

12. Gallagher and Thordason, *Design Thinking for School Leaders*, 5.

13. Gerzon, *Leadership through Conflict*, 7.

14. Gallagher and Thordason, *Design Thinking for School Leaders*, 12.

15. Heath and Heath, *Switch: How to Change Things When Change Is Hard* (New York: Broadway Books, 2010), 7. The Heath brothers attribute this metaphor to the work of Jonathan Haidt in *The Happiness Hypothesis: Finding Modern Trust in Ancient Wisdom* (New York: Basic Books, 2006).

16. Heath and Heath, *Switch*.

17. Hyatt, "Bad Decisions Don't Just Happen," Michaelhyatt.com, August 10, 2020, https://michaelhyatt.com/bad-decisions-dont-just-happen/?utm_source=feedburner&utm_medium=feed&utm_campaign=Feed%3A+michaelhyatt+%28Michael+Hyatt%29.

18. Runde and Flanagan, *Developing Conflict Competence* (San Francisco: Jossey-Bass, 2010), 4.

19. Dweck, "Growth Mindset," *Harvard Business Review*, January 13, 2016, https://leadlocal.global/wp-content/uploads/2016/12/Dweck-What-Having-a-%E2%80%9CGrowth-Mindset%E2%80%9D-Actually-Means-HBR.pdf.

20. Eddington et al., "Addressing Organizational Cultural Conflicts," *Negotiation and Conflict Management Research* 13, no. 3 (August 2020): 278, doi:10.1111/ncmr.12191.278.

21. Knowledge@Wharton, "Why You Need a 'Challenge Network,'" https://knowledge.wharton.upenn.edu/article/why-you-need-a-challenge-network/.

22. Donohoo, Hattie, and Eells, "The Power of Collective Efficacy"; Brown and Williams, "Creating Campus Teams That Perform after the Storm," *TEPSA Instructional Leader* 32, no. 3 (May 2019), www.tepsa.org/resource/creating-campus-teams-that-perform-after-the-storm.

23. T. Brown, *Change by Design*, 17.

24. Tyack and Tobin, "The 'Grammar' of Schooling," *American Educational Research Journal* 31, no. 3 (Fall 1994): 453–79. See chapter 2 of this book for further information.

25. Cited in Ghaffar, "Conflict in Schools," *Journal of Managerial Sciences* 3, no. 2 (July–December, 2009): 213, http://www.qurtuba.edu.pk/jms/default_files/JMS/3_2/05_ghaffar.pdf#:~:text=Conflict%20in%20Schools%3A%20Its%20Causes%20%26%20Management%20Strategies,among%20individuals%20and%20groups%20lead%20them%20to%20conflicts, emphasis added.

26. Gerzon, *Leadership through Conflict*, 7.

27. Craven, Fong, Lauricella, and Tan, "The Long Haul: How Leaders Can Shift Mindsets and Behaviors to Reopen Safely," McKinsey & Company, para. 17, www.mckinsey.com/business-functions/organization/our-insights/the-long-haul-how-leaders-can-shift-mindsets-and-behaviors-to-reopen-safely.

28. Gerzon, *Leadership through Conflict*, 164–65; Heath and Heath, *Switch*, 8.

29. Pentland. "The New Science of Building Great Teams," *Harvard Business Review*, para. 45, https://hbr.org/2012/04/the-new-science-of-building-great-teams.

30. Cited in de Jong, Kamsteeg, and Ybema, "Ethnographic Strategies for Making the Familiar Strange: Struggling with 'Distance' and 'Immersion' among Moroccan-Dutch Students," *Journal of Business Anthropology* 2, no. 2 (Fall 2013): 169.

31. Spencer, "The Launch Cycle: A K–12 Design Thinking Framework," para. 6, https://spencerauthor.com/the-launch-cycle/.

32. Conn and McLean, "Six Problem-Solving Mindsets for Very Uncertain Times," *McKinsey Quarterly*, September 15, 2020, para. 12, www.mckinsey.com/business-functions/strategy-and-corporate-finance/our-insights/six-problem-solving-mindsets-for-very-uncertain-times.

33. Conn and McLean, "Six Problem-Solving Mindsets," para. 16.

34. Conn and McLean, "Six Problem-Solving Mindsets," para. 2.

35. 500womenscientists.org. "Storytelling: Central to Human Experience," para. 4, https://500womenscientists.org/updates/2017/7/31/storytelling-human-experience.

36. DeVos, "Design Problem Statements—What They Are and How to Frame Them," Toptal, para. 26, www.toptal.com/designers/product-design/design-problem-statement.

37. Dam and Siang, "Stage 2 in the Design Thinking Process: Define the Problem and Interpret the Results," paras. 6–10.

38. Gallagher and Thordarson, *Design Thinking for School Leaders*, 44.

39. Heath and Heath, *Switch*, 74.

40. Gallagher and Thordarson, *Design Thinking for School Leaders*, 54.

41. Frey, "The 7 All-Time Greatest Ideation Techniques," Innovation Management, May 30, 2013, para. 22, https://innovationmanagement.se/2013/05/30/the-7-all-time-greatest-ideation-techniques/.

42. Burkus, "How Teams Should Make Decisions," Davidburkus.com, para. 11, https://davidburkus.com/2020/11/how-teams-should-make-decisions/.

Chapter Five

The Learning
Cycle . . . Creating Prototypes,
Testing Solutions, Getting Unstuck

Life is lived in perpetual beta.[1]

—Alyssa Gallagher and Kami Thordarson

Student discipline troubled Wanda Durite, principal of Ame High School. Actually, the source of her distress wasn't student behavior: Ame High School's student body consisted of normal adolescents occasionally testing boundaries and demonstrating the throes of teenage angst. She certainly didn't condone disrespect toward teachers and fighting, but to Wanda these were teachable moments amenable to a restorative justice approach such as mediation and nonpunitive restitution.

She seemed to be alone with this perspective though because her zero tolerance colleagues only wanted to know "Was the student suspended?" and "For how long?" They mocked the idea of alternatives to suspension, certain in their view that no accountability would invite worse behavior—and they had the superintendent of schools on their side. The school's diversity was a source of pride, which made data revealing that students of color were suspended at a disproportionate rate especially troubling. Wanda felt the inequities at Ame High were egregious but she could not get most of the staff or the superintendent to budge.

Middle schooler Anita Hope was a remarkably happy and industrious student . . . until young adolescence happened. Her parents observed with anguish as Anita's mood changed and even the most basic tasks like getting up in the morning and heading out the door to school became tumultuous struggles. Her school attendance sank together with her grades, which only recently had been a source of pride and a path to an outstanding college.

Anita's parents tried everything: grounding her over the weekend; parental controls on social media; confiscating her smartphone; psychotherapy; endless promises of concert tickets; even a raise in her allowance if they could just spot a glimmer of the Anita they once knew. For their part, Anita's teachers tried nurturing a relationship with her in the hallway between classes, instituted a behavior modification plan recommended by the school psychologist, occasionally assigned lunch detention, and emailed progress reports home every Friday.

Nothing was settled in a conference attended by Anita's parents and her teachers, guidance counselor, and assistant principal. The meeting, which began with each adult chronicling their efforts on Anita's behalf, prompted frustration and recriminations. When the school counselor, trying to be helpful, advised that "adolescence is a passing phase," her parents had a meltdown, replying with exasperation and tears, "We can't handle another year like this."

Chapter 4's introduction of design thinking described protocols enabling schools to reimagine vexing problems by thinking without the box. The process entails analyzing competing needs (empathy), pinpointing the problem (define), and generating creative solutions (ideate). While it may sound obvious, sometimes the problem is a lack of good solutions. That is where the next design thinking stage, prototype, enters the mix. Ideation results in recommendations for prototypes, defined as experimental models,[2] or proposed solutions that are actually implemented, which in turn leads to the next phase, test.

In *Improving Schools through Design Thinking*, Thomas Riddle explains the thought process.

> Understanding that prototypes may go through multiple iterations before a final product is produced encourages a mindset that's flexible, agile, and willing to work through the problem until the best result is obtained. So if input from teachers, students, and parents reveals that the new dress code has some flaws, instead of doubling down, we modify and revise based on their feedback until we develop the strongest solution.[3]

Given the prospect of multiple revisions, one may wonder whether design thinking is recursive or iterative. The distinction is revealing. Recursive signifies a repetitive process—think of the root word "recur." Iterative implies tweaking a solution to make improvements with each pass of the prototype-test cycle. In contrast to recursive revisiting, iterative connotes the process of change.

There's an analogy to scrambling eggs. Whisking eggs in a bowl is recursive: the chef applies the same process with each twitch of the hand until the eggs reaches the desired consistency. In an iterative process, the chef whisks the eggs, splashes milk to soften the texture, whisks some more, sprinkles an herb to enhance taste, whisks again, and so on. The design thinking process is sometimes illustrated in a linear fashion but a cyclical pattern more aptly depicts the evolutionary nature of design thinking (see figure 5.1).

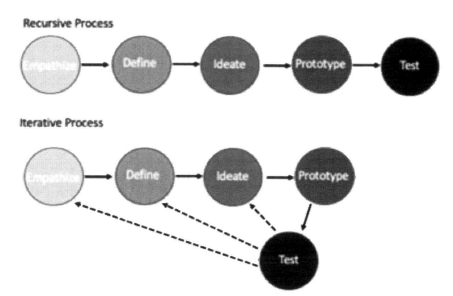

Figure 5.1.   Design Thinking: Recursive vs. Iterative Process

Design thinking literature generally associates prototypes with the development of a new product or an invention. For schools, a prototype may be a new curriculum or instructional practice; updated policies such as a code of conduct or homework guidelines; or modified procedures, for example, a plan to recruit diverse staff. Controversial issues present opportunities to follow design thinking protocols. In a clash between a faculty member and a parent over grades or disciplinary consequences, a prototype is a suggested resolution based on a shared understanding of the child and the school community's needs. Budget reduction decisions when resources are tight may result in a tentative agreement subject to the next phase in the design process, testing.

Table 5.1 presents opportunities for design thinking in schools. Each example meets the criteria for prototype development: following an assessment of stakeholder needs, a novel practice or product is generated and desired outcomes are identified. The problem under consideration is not simple or well defined, and the outcome is not assured. Dispelling the myth of the singular

Table 5.1.   Design Thinking Opportunities in Schools

Classroom Innovations	Instructional practices
	Curriculum initiatives
	Student assessment and grading
School Policies and	Student code of conduct
Procedures	Home and school intervention plan for an acting-out child
	Homework policies
	Access to advanced courses (gatekeeping and equity)
	Parent and community engagement
	Hiring procedures
	Diversity initiatives
Controversial Decisions	Teacher evaluation model
	Student class assignments
	Union contract negotiations
	Budget cuts
	Schedule changes

prototype, Riddle notes that proposed solutions are considered tentative at this stage and other options should still be on the table.[4]

An organization can study a problem forever, endlessly generating prototypes, never ready to launch. Gallagher and Thordarson assert that prototyping can alleviate "analysis paralysis,"[5] a proclivity to study a problem ad infinitum. Since a prototype is a tentative solution destined to be assessed in short order, there is less cause to be ponderous. Herein lies a conundrum, though, because what one person considers unnecessary detail or a stalling tactic evidences forethought and good planning to another. In excess, endless delays and rushed implementation are both detrimental.

There is no easy answer, so a school leader might lay out the issue to help both sides understand each other's perspectives and needs. The "Let's go ahead and start implementing" camp has a higher tolerance for uncertainty while the "Let's keep planning" contingent requires clarity. It's not unreasonable to want to know what you're getting into. That's the work of creating prototypes.

CREATING PROTOTYPES

Ame High School principal Durite cajoled enough teachers and parents to convene a discipline committee to review the student code of conduct. Student representatives were added as well. The committee soon found itself divided: a law-and-order contingent, consisting mostly of teachers, argued that strong consequences in the form of suspension were a deterrent, and because high school students were nearing adult age, it was appropriate to invoke substantial penalties for mistreatment of teachers and assaultive behavior. As one member stated, staff worried about a "tolerance for violence and mayhem" in a school that heretofore was considered safe.

Opponents vociferously contended that the school was violating the civil rights of children of color. They felt confident teenagers would respond to a rehabilitative approach and that the school was morally obligated to try. "We're treating children like criminals" was a frequent refrain. An emotional debate ensued as to whether differential disciplinary consequences were a manifestation of institutional racism or a series of individual circumstances, threatening to rip a fissure in the school community.

Adults participating in middle schooler Anita Hope's parent-teacher conference recognized they were losing her, and yet Anita defied, in every sense of the word, an array of interventions they had attempted. What did Anita need? When the social worker recommended weekly lunchtime counseling sessions, Anita's parents balked because socializing during lunch recess was the only school pastime she seemed to enjoy. The psychologist urged patience with the behavior modification plan, sparking the assistant principal to note that since the plan was adopted, Anita's behavior had actually worsened.

The science teacher wanted to bond with Anita by inviting her to feed fish in the classroom aquarium, provoking a sneer from the self-proclaimed tough love social studies teacher. For their part, the parents fluctuated between expressing disappointment that the efforts of the school and an outside psychotherapist were fruitless and occasionally desperately suggesting it was time to explore enlisting Anita in military school.

The first step in design thinking, described in chapter 4, is for the discipline committee and participants in Anita's parent-teacher conference to delineate the needs of the child and the school and then brainstorm a range of potential solutions. Next the focus shifts to the implementation phase as the group commits to a course of action (prototype) and creates a plan to assess the outcome (test).

Ideate, as explained in chapter 4, is an exercise in divergent thinking as the group conceives of multitudinous potential solutions. Once prototyping begins, the group shifts to convergent thinking: narrowing the options and settling on a few worth trying. At first blush, design thinking might appear to be a typical approach to problem solving: analyze the problem, devise a solution, implement the plan, assess results.

In fact, the iterative approach, especially the feedback loop from prototyping to testing then back to prototyping and testing again (and if necessary to the other three stages), is a consequential distinction. In this case, it offered the discipline committee and Anita's team multiple opportunities to resolve their differences and ultimately settle on a plan that might work.

Here's how prototyping proceeds.

❧ *Summarizing*—Recapping the consensus of the group or design team so far, the leader poses the following questions. (In the empathize, define, and ideate phases, many of these same issues were intensely studied.)

- What is the goal? For example, "We need a plan that will support the child completing homework with the parents and teachers on the same page" or "Our purpose is to develop a model for online instruction to enable learning at home while the building is closed due to the pandemic." A critical variable related to goal setting is time. The leader might urge an incremental approach, initially restricting the group to short-term objectives achievable in the near future: "Let's focus for now on helping the child complete math and English language arts homework." Similarly, the leader can break down a complex problem into component parts, first tackling the readily solvable, low-hanging fruit. A diversity committee might start with a goal to plan a multicultural curriculum before addressing discriminatory gatekeeping practices.
- What are the non-negotiables? In chapters 3 and 4, it was noted that the school leader must share non-negotiables, or parameters dictated by the leader, at the outset. As the group prepares to firm up prototypes, now is a suitable moment to recall ground rules.
- What components of a solution do we agree on? The standard in design thinking is commitment: to what elements of a solution are group members ready to commit themselves? Begin these meetings drawing a simple two-column chart on a marker board (see table 5.2). In the left column, list elicited points of agreement from the group. With the click of a smartphone camera, this T-chart becomes a written record of group decisions. If there is hesitation arriving at consensus, the leader may ask participants to

Table 5.2.   Decisions T-Chart

We agree . . .	To be determined . . .
•	•
•	•
•	•
•	•
•	•
•	•
•	•
•	•
•	•
•	•

hold up fingers indicating their level of concurrence: one finger indicates disagreement ("not *that* finger" may get a laugh); two fingers signify lukewarm support but "I can live with the solution"; and three fingers means wholehearted agreement. Jot the average number of fingers next to each bulleted item.

• What actions are to be determined? Addressing this question is the function of the right column of the T-chart. There is a different connotation in calling these matters "to be determined" rather than "disagreements." The former implies a sense of optimism that with further conversation the group will be able to settle the remaining issues. On the right side of the list, the three-finger exercise could indicate the level of priority or proximity to a resolution (near, far, or uncertain).

Often multiple prototypes are developed simultaneously either because a complex problem requires remediation on multiple fronts or because the outcome of each prototype is uncertain. A recent example of the latter was seen in the development of coronavirus vaccines. Pharmaceutical companies devised diverse prototypes: Pfizer and Moderna tested new mRNA technology; AstraZeneca and Johnson and Johnson advanced two different vector vaccines; and Merck's vaccination model was abandoned after clinical trials. With results indeterminable at the outset, simultaneous trials of several prototypes ultimately benefited public health.

Both discipline consequences at Ame High School and Anita Hope's recalcitrance are candidates for generating multiple prototypes, testing the effectiveness of each one, then making adjustments or disbanding solutions that are not effective. The role of the school leader once the T-chart is completed is to encourage design team members to adopt a design thinking mindset, replacing their predetermined convictions with an openness to experimentation followed by assessment.

As noted previously, confirmation bias is the tendency to favor information that confirms one's pre-existing beliefs while disregarding contradictory evidence. Therein lies the problem in countless meetings: each side is unshakably convinced they are right. In these later stages, design thinking has the capacity to shift the central question from divisive, "Who's right?" (a relationship issue), to collaborative, "What works?" and "How will we know?" (task and process features of the problem).

🖋 *Document Decisions*—Once the prototype is completed, document the substance, the assessment method, and plans for follow-up communication. Documentation may take the form of committee minutes, the first draft of a curriculum guide or policy statement, or a school counselor writing an email to a parent after a conference: "I enjoyed our meeting. We're hopeful that the weekly progress report we'll send home Fridays, and the reward system you're planning at home, will reinforce better homework habits. We hope to hear good news when we check in two weeks from now."

❦ *Don't Let the Perfect Be the Enemy of the Good*—Gallagher and Thordarson pose a query for design thinking practitioners: "Are you more likely to provide honest feedback to someone who presents you with a draft or to someone who presents you with a very slick digital solution?"[6] This rhetorical question is a reminder that the purpose of a prototype is to test and tweak a possible remedy with the underlying premise that stakeholders are searching for a solution together.

An article in *Harvard Business Review* made the same point: "Companies often regard prototyping as a process of fine-tuning a product or service that has already largely been developed. But in design thinking, prototyping is carried out on far-from-finished products. It's about users' iterative experiences with a work in progress."[7]

❦ *The Word "Pilot" Is a School Leader's Friend*—A central characteristic of the design thinking mindset is an inclination toward the tentative and short term: "It's just a pilot we're attempting for a limited time while we determine how well it works." There is less pressure, and therefore less dissension, accompanying decisions reached through the design thinking process because reconsideration will follow in the testing phase. Participants are reassured their voices will continue to be heard in an ongoing conversation. Consider these examples.

- (For a design team meeting) "Before we break up, let's set a date to meet a month from now to check in." "Talk to your colleagues. Find out what they think of our plan since they're the ones impacted." "Let me know if you have ideas for improvements, and you probably will. I'll put them on the agenda of our next meeting." "Remember, we are entering the pilot phase. Our work is by no means finished."
- (For a parent-teacher conference) "Call me in two weeks or shoot me an email to let me know how your child has been feeling about school." "Talk to your child tonight about our plan and let me know tomorrow what he says." "We agreed to try this. The next couple of weeks will be a trial period."

A second implication of a pilot, in addition to a test of limited duration, is limited scope. Rather than implementation targeting the entire school, one grade may attempt the new model or a handful of classrooms may be willing to be pioneers. After a suitable interval of data collection and analysis, and if the first adopters react positively, the program may be expanded with stronger support.

TESTING

In the test phase, the design thinking process enters a feedback loop cycling from prototype to test to another prototype and test, and back and forth, evaluating and consequently modifying the model with each go around. This approach may seem sensible enough but it's usually not how schools operate. Instead a committee convenes, promulgates a new program or policy, and then disbands once the initiatives are implemented: the work is done. Committee members typically say their goodbyes without committing themselves to a specific timeline or set of criteria to assess the outcome of their work and glean long-term lessons from implementation.

The design process exposes multiple fallacies in this line of thinking: without feedback, there is no sure means of evaluating the impact of decisions. Delaying evaluation until an indefinite time in the future negates the capacity to change course quickly in case an outcome is less than hoped. Deferring or neglecting the testing phase implies a certain hubris. There is an implicit denial of the wisdom conveyed in Robert Burn's poem that "the best laid schemes o' *Mice* an' *Men* / Gang aft agley [Go oft awry]."

In *Solving Team Conflicts with Design Thinking*, Rubio describes the benefit of testing vis-à-vis conflict resolution.

> Sometimes, conflict arises when individuals think that their solutions are the best, thus making measurement of idea-relevance a subjective process. However, through a well-thought experimentation process, where appropriate success measures are set up from the onset in order to validate initial assumptions, more objective results will determine whether an idea is suitable or not.[8]

Testing affords an opportunity for a fractious group to at least agree on desirable outcomes, determine the degree to which those outcomes have been reached, and commit themselves to continuous improvement until their goal is achieved.

❧ *Rapid Learning Cycles*—A central tenet of testing is the notion of rapid learning cycles. Testing is only effective to the extent data are regularly collected and scrutinized, which requires constant cycles of implementation, data gathering, analysis, and program modification. Experience leads to a caution: in schools, an interval of time is generally required for an intervention to take effect. Immediate data collection is useful to establish a baseline, but expecting instant results defies the incremental nature of school change.

❧ *Striking a Balance*—The first order of business is to decide on the assessment criteria. How will the design team know whether it is making progress toward its goal? Notice that the question implies formative assessment: the task at this stage is to determine whether there has been movement in the right direction. The essence of the testing phase is to evaluate the viability of a solution while it is still being forged. Your GPS has not yet declared you've reached your destination, you just want the electronic voice to proclaim you're on course!

Gallagher and Thordarson emphasize, "The most important piece of testing is the feedback process. In order to make changes to your idea, you need to know which parts of your prototype are meeting the needs of your people and which parts are not."[9] Key questions, they suggest, are "What worked? What didn't? What can be improved?"[10] Khalil and Kier advise the object of feedback is to "reassess alignment between problem, strategy and intended outcome."[11]

There is a balance between insufficient measures to evaluate the effectiveness of an initiative and having too many or overly complex assessments. Multiple means of assessment are helpful but not so many that evaluation per se dominates attention. Assessments need not meet the rigor of academic research; "utilitarian" is an apt descriptive term here. Principles of action research better reflect the ad hoc, informal nature of data collection and analysis at this stage. Eileen Ferrance, formerly of Brown University's Education Alliance, delineates what action research is and what it is *not*: "Often, action research is a collaborative activity among colleagues searching for solutions to everyday, real problems experienced in schools."[12]

Ferrance goes on to say, "Action research is not about doing research on or about people, or finding all available information on a topic looking for the correct answers. It involves people working to improve their skills, techniques, and strategies. Action research is not about learning why we do certain things, but rather how we can do things better."[13]

❧ *Naturalistic Data Collection*—Use pre-existing assessments as much as possible, and if new data collection is necessary, make the procedure as non-invasive as possible. "Testing," according to Gallagher and Thordarson, "can be as simple as sharing a rapidly made prototype with a small group or trying out a new schedule for a few weeks."[14] Simple checklists and tallies may work too. As Sagor explains in connection with his model of the process,

> For the harried and overworked teacher, "data collection" can appear to be the most intimidating aspect of the entire seven-step action research process. The question I am repeatedly asked, "Where will I find the time and expertise to develop valid and reliable instruments for data collection?" gives voice to a realistic fear regarding time management. Fortunately, classrooms and schools are, by their nature, data-rich environments. Each day a child is in class, he or she is producing or not producing work, is interacting productively with classmates or experiencing difficulties in social situations, and is completing assignments proficiently or poorly.[15]

Table 5.3. Examples of Data in the Testing Phase

Classroom Innovation	School Policies and Procedures	Controversial Issues
Teacher and student surveys	Teacher and student attendance data	Teacher year-end rating data
Practitioner interviews		
Longitudinal data	Homework completion rate in teacher gradebook	Actual budget expenditures vs. allocations
Anecdotal classroom accounts		
Analysis of student work	Analysis of student work	Per-student cost of programs
Observation reports	Suspension and detention frequency data	
Rubrics		Pre- and post-surveys
Formal and informal student assessment data	Community surveys	Root cause analysis
	Comparisons with other schools	Cost and benefit evaluation
	Teacher and administrator turnover data	

More examples are displayed in table 5.3.

🔖 *Scaling or Pivoting*—As a result of assessment, design thinking anticipates alternative outcomes: scaling or pivoting. If data indicate the prototype generated the desired results, then the solution can be scaled, that is, expanded beyond the limited scope of the pilot. Pivoting is the antithesis. Rubio explains, "Pivoting means that the outcomes do not prove the initial assumptions, therefore [the prototype] is not suitable as an answer to current problems or opportunities."[16]

Much has been written in the literature describing the capacity of successful organizations in all fields to accept risks and adapt to inevitable missteps in the process of improvement. Chapter 3 describes the advantageous effect of a leader's belief that errors pose learning opportunities. Riddle's *Improving Schools through Design Thinking* attests to the phenomenon.

> Too often, if a new idea doesn't work flawlessly right out of the gate, it's quickly labeled a failure. When this happens (and it will), don't think of it as failing, think of it as failing forward—an outlook which recognizes that if you don't give up, if you learn from the mistakes you made, you're better positioned to create a stronger solution next time. Make your course corrections based on observation and feedback, then roll out Version Two.[17]

Behal and Moore call this orientation "productive failure." It's an integral tenet in the culture of design thinking organizations.[18]

🔖 *Finally, Process the Process*—The last step facilitates the integration of collaborative behaviors and norms in school culture, which is the ultimate objective of conflict-agility practices. Before the design team disbands, it is worthwhile to debrief the process. "How would you describe our journey together?" "What were the bumps in the road and how did we get past them?" "What did we learn about each other?" These questions help group members appreciate the process; they enable members to improve on group dynamics in the future; and they encourage acceptance of conflict-agility as a part of "the way we do things around here."

Ame High's discipline committee engaged in contentious debate between the law-and-order contingent proposing strict disciplinary response to behavior infractions and the rehabilitation camp, including Principal Durite, advocating for restorative justice. To break the logjam, Wanda turned to design thinking. She reassured the committee that both sides had valid arguments: everyone could agree that effective discipline was necessary to maintain an orderly climate conducive to learning. On the other hand, everyone was disturbed by the data she shared showing children of color were disproportionately suspended.

After completing its initial design work, the committee agreed to a prototype restorative justice program that would be implemented on a limited basis for freshmen and sophomores in the next semester. The design team would continue to meet to assess whether the new initiative succeeded in resolving student conflicts without exacerbating inappropriate behavior. Wanda was satisfied. The prototype might be a step in the right direction, and the committee had launched a worthwhile conversation in the school community about equity and student responsibility.

Anita Hope's parents and teachers were also stymied. Privately, the school psychologist and assistant principal felt Anita was one of the most recalcitrant students they had encountered in decades of middle school—and they had seen a lot. The group decided they needed more information. Anita's parents would consult with her outside therapist (and check on military school tuition too).

The teachers would convene another team meeting, this time with Anita in attendance. They would ask her to describe her experience in recent weeks and coax her to name rewards she might enjoy—part of a revised behavior modification plan with the child's participation. Upon returning to the office, the assistant principal began typing an email to the adults in Anita's life, thanking them for caring, reiterating the plan, and reminding them about a follow-up meeting in two weeks. "We've got this," the assistant principal reassured the group in closing.

GETTING UNSTUCK

In writing this book, one of our concerns was that we might convey the false impression that remedies to perplexing and perpetual conflict are formulaic, as if following a six-step (or six-chapter) program were sure to dissipate discord. Would that it were so simple. In fact, there are higher degrees of conflict intensity, intransigently difficult people, vested political interests, and abysmally dysfunctional organization dynamics. Runde and Flanagan posit five ascending levels of conflict intensity from differences and misunderstandings in which parties differ but feel no discomfort to disagreements, discord, and polarization characterized by increasing animosity.[19]

Perceptions of school culture are shaped by the outcome of conflicts in which the school was plagued by dissension. Ask around a school: conflicts encountered in the past are remembered equally for the issues and the residue, that is, how or whether the matter was ultimately resolved. For example,

- "The contract was settled but hard feelings remain that still haunt day-to-day relationships."
- "The community never moved past the redistricting proposal. Five years later residents still vociferously argue at board meetings and cocktail parties and we still haven't figured out what to do about our overcrowded schools."

Former combatants, reflecting back, may believe "Those were tough times, but we came together and moved forward" or they might feel yesterday's conflict was yet another example of battle lines immutably drawn.

Imagine you've followed the practices recommended in this book. You're an exemplary leader exuding trustworthy qualities and a mediator capable of coalescing an organization in productive dialogue. You model risk taking and disagreement without dissension and you've employed the design thinking process to generate without-the-box solutions. Still the design team is unable to make progress because it cannot agree on a prototype to implement and test. Enmeshed in conflict, how does the group become untangled?

🌡 *Set Realistic Expectations*—Instill in the group recognition that long-standing conflict is usually no fluke: there is usually a good reason why parties disagree. The cause of conflict might be the result of newly imposed state or federal laws, of participants advocating divergent interests, or of a lack of universally accepted best practice. Conflict is a normal state of human affairs. As Uline, Tschannen-Moran, and Perez recognize, "conflict is present within our schools whether we like it or not."[20] The role of the school leader, as chapter 3 explained, is to help participants accept disagreement without discord.

❧ *Decide How to Decide*—In *The Role of Conflict in Design*, Brown re-marks, "There are two parts to any design decision: the *content* of the deci-sion and the *method* used to make the decision."[21] If they can't agree on the substance of the issue, at least the design team might reach consensus on a path forward or at least one or two next steps. If not the *what*, at least the *how*. "With school opening next week, we need to implement the curriculum but we'll organize a committee to get feedback and revise" or "Let's meet Wednesdays during lunchtime to work out the wording of the new policy. I'll bring snacks."

In deciding how to decide, what else does the group need to move forward? More information might reveal a novel solution. This tactic does not imply the proverbial fishing expedition without purpose or direction. Specify the information needed, how the information will help the group progress, and set a deadline to reconvene. For example, "We need to study assessment options for teacher performance evaluation. I'll poll schools in the county to ask what others are doing" or "Let's check with the school psychologist and the child's outside therapist to ascertain their advice. Then we'll reconvene next week."

❧ *Think Small*—Divide and conquer the problem (but not the people) by breaking it down and solving it in parts. Perhaps, as suggested earlier, pick the low-hanging fruit most amenable to remedy and give your group time to build conflict-agility skills and confidence in group problem solving. Or start with only one manifestation of the problem, realizing that to get from A to Z you need to travel through points B, C, and D, and so forth.

If your committee revising the code of conduct is arguing relentlessly over whether it is appropriate to suspend students from extracurricular sports as a consequence of in-classroom behavior, switch to another section of the code. The design thinking model inherently suggests another think-small tactic: generate short-term pilot studies using an iterative approach rather than per-manent answers. Accept that the initial solution will be imperfect and require revisiting.

❧ *Think Big*—Sometimes the obstacle is the opposite: the group might ben-efit by broadening its perspective. Sixth-grade teachers, for example, might be stuck deciding which model of student desks to purchase: traditional desk-tops or college-style folding tablets. They're not considering how classroom design has been revolutionized to accommodate today's information age and student-centered learning or researching nonstandard alternatives like stand-ing desks. Schools often crawl through the weeds to find answers rather than gaze toward the sky.

To look beyond self-imposed constraints, encourage the design team to use their BRAIN.

- **B**rainstorm three more options. Groups often discontinue the creative thought process after identifying just one solution.
- **R**oleplay how a well-respected figure might approach the problem. For example, what might Carol Dweck or Nelson Mandela advise?
- Keep in mind that **A**ssumptions that limit perspectives and alternatives must be examined. Conduct an assumptions audit.
- Remember that **I**deal solutions—if money, time, and any other limitation are disregarded—widen the range of possibilities.
- Seek **N**ovelty: What has no other school dared to do?

DIFFICULT PEOPLE

Reviewing the appointment calendar at the beginning of every month, the only meeting the principal, Ed Kadem, dreads is the union rep meeting. He ponders which activity he looks forward to *less*: teacher union representatives gathered around his conference table to gripe or dental check ups.

Ten times each school year, union representatives arrive with a sheaf of complaints ranging from petty to irresolvable. Administrative response, or lack thereof, to student misbehavior is a recurring theme: So-and-so was sent to the office but "nothing happened." Reports of low faculty morale, late-night parent emails, and allegations that administrators only care about standardized test scores spark tense recriminations.

Ed privately likens these meetings to competitive tennis: teacher representatives served a hot shot over the net, he or the assistant principal returned the volley, and so began the back and forth, month after month, year after year. As he scans the faces around the table, he realizes the representatives are not monolithic. He feels he enjoys a positive relationship with five out of six . . . except for that hour beginning at 3:00 p.m. on the first Wednesday of every month.

Then there's Ina Huff. Ed can't fathom why the teachers would elect their most egregiously unprofessional colleague to represent them. Largely disinterested in the classroom, Ina's demeanor during monthly rep and faculty meetings turns acerbic. Ed wishes he could cancel the monthly meeting but unfortunately, it is mandated by contract. He will just have to tolerate it. Like a visit to the dentist.

When educators think of conflict in schools, most likely they attribute the cause to people like Ina Huff, or a clash between Ina and an obstinate principal. Chapter 2 cited Jehn's conception of three types of conflict: relationship, task, and process.[22] People often bring relationship issues to the fore, and these are often the most difficult to remedy.

Runde and Flanagan posit two types of discord: cognitive and affective, the latter calling to mind Ina.[23] Or as Uline, Tschannen-Moran, and Perez succinctly state, "The problem is that in most cases participants' ability to stimulate conflict outstrips their knowledge of how to manage its effects."[24]

Where do relationship or affective issues come from? There are many potential causes including the emotional baggage everyone carries, prior experiences in the workplace, feelings about authority, and relationships among the parties involved. Thorough treatment of relationship and affective conflicts would require volumes much less finding remedies. The immediate challenge facing a school leader like Ed confronting an intractable adult is to extricate the noxious relationship from the decision-making process. Three proven strategies are described below.

⚜ *Don't Give Them Power*—Todd Whitaker, author of *Dealing with Difficult Teachers*, asserts, "One of the faults in education and educational leadership is that we give too much power to these difficult people."[25] He shares an illustrative account of a dedicated teacher asking what Whitaker would do because a notoriously resistant colleague was missing from a productive summer workshop he was leading. Whitaker's response? "I would praise the Lord."[26]

While soliciting disaffected voices is an effective conflict remediation strategy repeatedly suggested in this book, there are limitations, an example being one cantankerous person blocking consensus among the remaining staff. Seth advised teachers inquiring about "willfully unwilling" colleagues in circumstances similar to Whitaker's story, "We're not going to wait for everyone to board the bus before we leave the station."

⚜ *Be the Adult in the Room*—The vast majority of faculty members are well-meaning and are uncomfortable with the Ina Huffs of this world. Even if they remain silent, they are undoubtedly observing interactions and noticing the leader's response. Getting into shouting matches or exchanging accusations and barbs engulfs the leader in the most ruinous form of conflict. Instead, play a long game: shift the climate surrounding conflict by modeling respect and civility, laying the groundwork for cultural change.

⚜ *Worse Comes to Worst*—Uline, Tschannen-Moran, and Perez urge drawing boundaries, or "maintain[ing] conflict at some optimal level . . . to keep participants' responses appropriate and productive."[27] On rare occasion, it may be necessary to halt a meeting or conversation in the name of setting respectful limits and avoiding further harm. Runde and Flanagan suggest that leaders call time-out when necessary, a strategy offering three benefits.[28]

1. Separation allow you to cool down and slow a response because it is divorced from the heat of the moment.

2. A break offers all parties an opportunity for reflection on what is working and not working.
3. Once strong emotions subside and a better climate is established, the next step is to reengage, perhaps clearing the air and reframing the issue.

Principal Kadem decides it is time for a heart-to-heart talk with Ina. After several long talks with his partner, the feeling that Ina is his nemesis is beginning to fade, and he resolves to broach the possibility of improving their relationship. As his partner suggests, "Someone needs to be the adult in the room" and in this case, seek a course correction. But how to begin?

Ed gives considerable thought to the conversation in advance. Rather than summon Ina to an appointment in his office, he will approach Ina alone in her classroom in a casual and non-threatening manner, offer an olive branch in the form of her favorite brand of coffee, and begin, "Ina, can we talk for a few minutes?" He will express his hope to turn a page on their relationship with her input, and ask when and where they might continue talking. "I don't expect one cup of coffee will revive our relationship," he'll conclude the session. "I'm hoping we'll look back one day and say it was a start."

CHAPTER SUMMARY

Prototypes provide a path for addressing conflict productively. A prototype is essentially an experiment awaiting the results of data to assess its effectiveness and determine whether refinements will yield further improvement. Riddle suggests perhaps the most salient benefit: "Design thinking encourages a bias toward action and, because of its reliance on rapid prototyping, frees practitioners to embrace the notion of failing forward because it's okay to make mistakes—that's where breakthrough ideas are born."[29] Design thinking emphasizes objective verification and collectively held standards for success.

The iterative nature of prototyping and testing is key: a rapid learning cycle engages the group in a continuous process of evaluation and revision. The evolutionary nature of prototyping and testing is contrary to standard school practice since committees typically disband once a plan reaches the implementation phase. The notion of a pilot program to be revisited frees participants to deviate from unshakeable convictions. Strategies to get unstuck include thinking small, zooming in on the most solvable elements of a problem, and thinking big by finding a more imaginative tact.

CONTEMPLATING CONFLICT

Here are some questions for your consideration as you think about the contents of this chapter.

1. What are two ideas you might borrow from the prototype-test process over the next week?
2. Name three sources of data your school already collects that would be most applicable in solving a contentious issue your school is now experiencing.
3. Identify a problem in your school. Would it be more productive to think small or think big?
4. To what extent does the quote "Life is lived in perpetual beta"[30] describe your personal or professional life?

NOTES

1. Gallagher and Thordarson, *Design Thinking for School Leaders: Five Roles and Mindsets That Ignite Positive Change* (Alexandria, Virginia: Association for Supervision and Curriculum Development, 2018), 11.

2. Interaction Design Foundation, "What Is Prototyping?" www.interaction -design.org/literature/topics/prototyping.

3. Riddle, "Improving Schools through Design Thinking," Edutopia, February 3, 2016, www.edutopia.org/blog/improving-schools-through-design-thinking-thomas -riddle.para. 7.

4. Riddle, "Improving Schools through Design Thinking," para 7.

5. Gallagher and Thordarson, *Design Thinking for School Leaders*, 129.

6. Gallagher and Thordarson, *Design Thinking for School Leaders*, 129.

7. Leidtka, "Why Design Thinking Works," *Harvard Business Review* (September–October, 2018), https://hbr.org/2018/09/why-design-thinking-works, para. 35.

8. Rubio, "Solving Team's Conflict with Design Thinking," LinkedIn, June 8, 2016, www.linkedin.com/pulse/solving-teams-conflicts-design-thinking-enrique -rubio, para. 12.

9. Gallagher and Thordarson, *Design Thinking for School Leaders*, 130.

10. Gallagher and Thordarson, *Design Thinking for School Leaders*, 130.

11. Khalil and Kier, "Equity-Centered Design Thinking in STEM Instructional Leadership," *Journal of Cases in Educational Leadership* 24, no. 1 (March 2021): 77.

12. Ferrance, *Action Research* (Providence, RI: Northeast and Islands Regional Education Laboratory, 2000), introduction.

13. Ferrance, *Action Research*, 2–3.

14. Gallagher and Thordarson, *Design Thinking for School Leaders*, 130.

15. Sagor, *Guiding School Improvement with Action Research* (Alexandria, VA: Association for Supervision and Curriculum Development, 2000), 5.

16. Rubio, "Solving Team's Conflict with Design Thinking," para. 13.

17. Riddle, "Improving Schools through Design Thinking," para. 8.

18. Behal and Moore, "Design Thinking and Culture Change," Mindhatch Insights, www.mindhatchllc.com/design-thinking-organizational-culture-change/.

19. Runde and Flanagan, *Building Conflict Competent Teams: How You and Your Organization Can Manage Conflict Effectively* (San Francisco: Jossey-Bass, 2007), 78–86.

20. Uline, Tschannen-Moran, and Perez, "Constructive Conflict," *Teachers College Record* 105, no. 5 (June 2003): 782.

21. Brown, *Designing Together: The Collaboration and Conflict Management Handbook for Creative Professionals* (Indianapolis, IN: Peachpit Press, 2013), 44.

22. Jehn, Greer, Levine, and Szulanski, "The Effects of Conflict Types, Dimensions, and Emergent States on Group Outcomes," *Group Decision and Negotiation* 17, no. 6 (November 2008): 465–95, doi:10.1007/s10726-008-9107-0.

23. Runde and Flanagan, *Becoming a Conflict-Competent Leader*, 26–27.

24. Uline, Tschannen-Moran, and Perez, "Constructive Conflict," 810.

25. Whitaker, *Dealing with Difficult Teachers*, 2nd ed. (Larchmont, NY: Eye on Education, 2002), 19.

26. Whitaker, *Dealing with Difficult Teachers*, 20.

27. Uline, Tschannen-Moran, and Perez, "Constructive Conflict," 799.

28. Runde and Flanagan, *Building Conflict Competent Teams*, 137–40.

29. Riddle, "Improving Schools through Design Thinking," para. 1.

30. Gallagher and Thordarson, *Design Thinking for School Leaders*, 11.

Chapter Six

Looking Backward, Moving Forward

If we seek to "win" the conflict, we will ultimately lose. But if we seek to transform it, we will neither win nor lose but will find opportunities in our differences that go far beyond our imagination.[1]

—Mark Gerzon

This book began by asserting that conflict in schools is inevitable and that viewing it only as an us-versus-them situation blinds principals and other school leaders to the possibility that conflict, when properly addressed, can serve as the impetus to resolve seemingly intractable, wicked problems. But the value of the process presented throughout this book goes far beyond solving the issues of the moment: the strategies described in the preceding chapters develop the conflict-agility schools and school leaders need to surmount both short- and long-term challenges and promote continuous improvement.

Schools that address conflict successfully can focus more intently on their mission and the work required to achieve it, a phenomenon Fullan and Quinn call "coherence."[2] They can similarly increase capacity for problem solving in all aspects of school operation, maintain positive connections among stakeholders, enhance school leadership, and improve school culture and climate. In the end, students will learn more, feel a stronger sense of community, and enjoy school life more fully if the adults around them can iron out their differences by reaching across the proverbial aisle to engage in constructive dialogue just as they hope to see in classrooms.

It may be difficult to consider conflict as an ally rather than an impediment. Indeed, personal experiences with the stresses and ill will (and sometimes ill health) associated with conflict make it difficult to see it from a different perspective. In organizational terms, conflict has traditionally been viewed as a negative, a leadership failure, an indicator that something is amiss. Conflict, when poorly addressed, can cripple interpersonal relationships, create a negative climate, and constrain innovation.

Principals report a significant level of discomfort with conflict and feel unprepared to address it on the job.[3] Distaste for conflict, coupled with concerns that divisiveness will disrupt school activities, add another set of pressures to already overburdened school leaders who have responsibility for everything that takes place within their school buildings.

Earlier chapters also cited research that suggests teachers and principals have very different views of their role in handling conflict, with teachers voicing criticism of their school leaders' actions and principals offering positive views of their efforts.[4] In addition, advances in technology have increased the potential for conflict among all members of the school community, with social media providing a potent vehicle for divisive rhetoric, personal attacks, misinterpretation of messages, and restriction of the field of vision only to groups, websites, or posts that support one's point of view.

Given the negative experiences and associations coupled with our notions of conflict, it is hardly surprising that avoidance or attack (the first two *A*s) are often the initial response of school leaders and other stakeholders. While addressing every conflict that arises is neither practical nor desirable, ignoring them or squashing them is ineffective as well.

Researchers have found that unaddressed conflict can reduce organizational productivity.[5] The stress that accompanies conflict can wreak havoc with emotions and destroy collegiality and friendships.[6] Stress also constrains clear thinking as fight-or-flight reactions (the Heath brothers' elephant) overpower logic and flexible thinking (the Heath brothers' rider).[7]

When deep discord exists, stakeholders taking different sides of an argument feel alienated from each other and become emotionally distanced from their schools, factors that can reduce the sense of psychological ownership that contributes to organizational vitality.[8] Fear of losing can harden battle lines, shut down communication, and create psychic wounds that persist for a long time. Mark Gerzon, long recognized for his role in resolving conflicts, succinctly captures these dark outcomes by concluding, "Conflicts usually consist of genuine differences compounded by stuck positions, fixed attitudes, hardened identities, and closed hearts."[9]

The difficulty of addressing conflict successfully can easily shift focus from long-term results to a quick fix. Such efforts are unlikely to bear fruit. Superficial solutions provide temporary relief at best, leaving underlying issues only to fester and then return with greater intensity at a later date. Top-down solutions arouse suspicion and resistance and seem out of touch with trends toward distributed leadership and shared decision making. Previously tried remedies, repackaged and redeployed, exacerbate frustrations and arouse concerns about the school's ability to adapt to changing circumstances.

Compromise too may fail to address the real issues that keep the conflict alive as all parties privy to the settlement emerge with a less-than-satisfying piece of what was desired. Temporarily the school may return to some level of equilibrium as people hope that their voices have been heard, their messages understood.

Over time, however, the situation deteriorates: some become resentful, others become apathetic. Trust withers. The long-standing result is a school that lacks sufficient capabilities—conflict-agility—to address the clashes that inevitably emerge or reemerge because of the complexity of schooling and the values, beliefs, and yes, biases of its stakeholders and the ever-changing educational environment. Toxicity finds it easy to thrive in such circumstances, and the poison can rapidly spread to relationships, tasks, policies, and procedures previously uncontested.

Conflict-agility developed through design thinking builds an ongoing capacity for problem solving when solutions are not readily apparent or within easy reach. It identifies conflict not as something to be ignored or suppressed but rather as a part of the pattern of school life that can facilitate both organizational development and personal growth.

By using the strategies of design thinking, principals and other school leaders can help their communities develop practices, strategies, and dispositions that become part of organizational culture and thereby serve as the accepted method for resolving "incompatibility, disagreement, or dissonance"[10] among individuals or groups without creating a residue of rancor. Instead of jumping from one issue to the next, leaders can use these strategies to achieve Gerzon's lofty goal of fixing the process not simply the current problem.[11]

DESIGN THINKING, CONFLICT-AGILITY, AND SCHOOL CAPACITY

How does design thinking contribute to the achievement of these ambitious aims? First, it provides a structure that can serve as what Heifetz and Linsky call "a holding environment."[12] A holding environment consists of a physical, virtual, or figurative space where expectations and procedures are in place for handling the volatile emotions associated with conflict in a safe manner.

Holding environments fortify social ties. They offer settings where grievances can be aired, sensitive topics explored, and patience developed to handle the halting progress typical of work on sensitive topics. In a holding environment, members of the school community can discuss questions that arouse strong feelings ranging from localized, time-bound concerns like duty assignments to broad issues like the inequitable treatment of different groups of students.

The ground rules for design thinking, which provide both flexibility and a set of protocols that facilitate productive engagement, provide the needed conditions for such safe debate. Reflection serves as a cornerstone of the process: once embedded as a valued practice, it can enable stakeholders to recognize other aspects of school life when their own cognitive biases may interfere with the analysis of the situation or when their emotions may cloud judgment.

Reflection also operates as a brake on the impulse to find quick fixes. School community members who understand the value of reflection in problem solving become skillful at following Runde and Flanagan's advice to cool down and slow down during times of difficulty.[13] Design thinking's consistent emphasis on finding practical solutions for divisive issues also offers a strategy useful for reducing the emotional temperature of debate by separating interpersonal concerns, which are unlikely to lead stakeholders down useful paths from the task or process in which disagreement is rooted.[14] Better decisions result.

Design thinking additionally builds experience with—and confidence in—an iterative approach to important issues in which participants review and re-vise ideas as new information becomes available, new insights are generated, feedback is received, and model solutions are collaboratively constructed, tested, and evaluated. The use of prototyping, or piloting in common school language, provides a mechanism for advancing ideas in an atmosphere of psychological safety with the understanding that the model will be revisited and revised as needed before advancing to full implementation.

Empathy drives design thinking and is vital to long-term school success. The information gathering that takes place during the empathize stage of the design process requires careful attention to all those whose interests are involved with the added step for schools of always seeking to prioritize the student perspective and the impact on student achievement and well-being. This process, coupled with critical self-reflection and group discussion, sensi-tizes participants to the viewpoints of others and serves as a vivid reminder of the value of shedding one's prejudices and preconceptions at the schoolhouse doors.

Deep engagement in empathy activities leads to a more inclusive perspec-tive on the needs and goals of different individuals or factions within (and outside) the school community. Empathy also erodes social boundaries and counteracts the tendency of schools, like other organizations, to create silos that constrain the development of shared understandings and unified action.

Once school community members develop their empathy skills and start looking at problematic situations from the inside out, they become much more aware of how they interact with others and how others see them. Most critically, they truly listen for understanding. They identify areas of agreement and resist the temptation to find flaws in the positions of others. Experience teaches them that discussion can accommodate multiple viewpoints without descending into bitterness. They use that understanding to create holistic perspectives and escape the tunnel vision that can derail even the most carefully planned initiatives.

As the capacity for empathy increases, defensiveness declines. Interpersonal rifts—relationship conflicts—take a back seat to the good of the whole. Stakeholders can then find the strength to confront difficult questions about their impact on students, their connections with others, the values and beliefs they hold dear, and the role of schooling in fulfilling the promise of democracy. With empathy, members of school communities can seek to bridge the divisions that separate them, address inequities, support families, and promote the growth of every student.

Experiences with design thinking demonstrate in dramatic fashion the value of what leadership consultant David Chrislip calls "the collaborative principle," which states, "If you bring *appropriate people* together in constructive ways with *reliable information*, they will create authentic vision and strategies for addressing the shared concerns of the organization or community."[15]As they work toward solutions, participants engage in collaborative exercises to organize and reflect on data and observations, bounce ideas off each other, and reach agreements about the issues under the issues.

Creative juices are stirred by learning to think without the box. Designers learn to ask good questions, ones that penetrate deeply beneath the surface as well as shift between wide-angle and telephoto lenses as they analyze problems. Schools can also adapt brainstorming and related techniques to situations outside the design process to encourage creative thinking, suspension of judgment, and risk taking.

Design thinking's focus on specific, school-based issues and its commitment to recognizing the needs and interests of stakeholders can help establish meaningful professional learning agendas for the faculty and school leaders alike. As part of the design process, schools may discover new topics for professional development or a need to revisit previous efforts. The localized context of such work makes it more likely that participants feel engaged in meaningful activities. It also embeds professional learning in the particular needs of the school, a best practice in professional development that makes it more likely innovations will last.[16]

The design process nurtures the conditions in which conflict-agile teams thrive. In 2012, Google began a study of its own operations to identify the ingredients that made some of its many teams more successful than others. The initiative, called Project Aristotle, conducted a multifaceted study that included a review of research, surveys, and interviews and a comprehensive analysis of Google team composition, behavior, and accomplishments.

The final report concluded that the membership of teams did not matter as much as the processes groups employed to address their goals.[17] Five team characteristics stood out and each has a parallel in the conflict-agility model as presented in table 6.1. Note too the parallels with Gerzon's time-tested strategies for conflict resolution, which emphasize the importance of holistic understandings of conflict and full commitment to addressing it.[18]

Table 6.1. Parallels between Project Aristotle Conclusions and Conflict-Agility

Team Characteristic	Conflict-Agility Element
Psychological safety	Holding environment
Dependability (Team members are reliable)	Group norms and processes requiring full commitment and interdependence of team members, much like what Gerzon terms "Presence"
Structure and clarity (Expectations for team and member performance)	Design brief to delineate goals and desired outcomes; shared leadership responsibilities to promote accountability of all participants; follow-up for recommendations for resolution to ensure plans are enacted
Meaning	Direct focus on stakeholder needs through empathize stage; attention addressed to assumptions, values, beliefs, and organizational culture, much like what Gerzon terms "integral vision"
Impact	Iterative process of prototype and test with feedback gathered at each stage; implementation of best model and continuous improvement of capacity

The use of design thinking principles and processes to address divisive issues also changes the way in which leadership is exercised in a school. As observers of schooling have noted, the role of the principal has expanded dramatically over the past few decades, today including a healthy dose of accountability for everything that takes place within the school community. In this environment, principals cannot be successful if they operate as the sole source of educational leadership in a school: they must share responsibilities with faculty.

Design thinking's commitment to respecting all perspectives regardless of role or status in the school community builds leadership skills and understanding among stakeholders. The organizational chart yields to decisions informed by critical reflection, wide-ranging discussion, and the consideration of data and other information gathered and contributed by participants.

Successful experience with discussions in which all parties have equal status in turn provides a model for distributing leadership throughout the school. School community members similarly gain experience in managing collaborative projects, setting goals, and assessing results. With practice and success, they also become more proficient communicators who share ideas effectively, receive feedback graciously, and model transparency.

The insights experienced by addressing wicked problems successfully helps school stakeholders develop more sophisticated perspectives on the challenge of change, and they come to understand how many aspects of school life are interconnected. With practice, they become more skillful at enlisting support and addressing questions (and resistance) from others. In this way, they learn that school improvement is above all a human rather than a technical process, and they discover first hand the validity of Michael Fullan's conclusion about change: "If relationships improve, things get better."[19]

Strengthened relationships also result from an increase in trust, one of the cornerstones of effective schools. Trust serves as a lubricant that facilitates interaction and sustains commitment to shared goals.[20] As every school leader can attest, developing trust is easier said than done—particularly when social tensions are rife.

As part of building a school's conflict-agility, principals promote trust through transparency, consistent application of the design process, and demonstrations of empathy. They demonstrate conflict-agile behavior, avoiding impulsive mistakes by ascending to the balcony when things get heated and taking a broader, less-volatile view of the factors involved in contentious situations.[21] They create the psychological safety of a holding environment, a space in which contrasting viewpoints are deemed essential for problem solving.

Leaders also display openness to new ideas, provide time for them to mature, respect informal leadership, and act with integrity by committing to the recommendations offered by the design team. When problems occur or errors are made, principals and other school leaders engage with stakeholders in efforts to improve outcomes and not assign blame. Perhaps most importantly, they seek to include those most marginalized, modeling the moral imperative of equity and demonstrating to all the practical value of "crowdsource[ing] ideas and strategies when designing and refining possible solutions."[22]

Improved relationships increase social capital, the bonds that cement sustained mutual engagement and cooperation. The bonds include parents, who come to recognize that their voices will be heard and appreciated and learn that touchy subjects can be addressed without toxicity. Pathways to resolving issues without hostility become more accessible for all and less likely to carry emotional baggage and defensiveness by all parties. Engaging others with respect and empowering stakeholders to make decisions reduces cynicism and increases morale.[23]

Conflict-agility requires a fundamentally different mindset compared to many schools' modus operandi. These diametrically opposite perspectives are delineated in table 6.2. The table's title, "The Conflict-Agility Mindset: This Not That," highlights the contrast. The conflict-agile school emphasizes

Table 6.2. The Conflict-Agility Mindset: This Not That

Conflict-Agility Mindset Exhibits This: Not That	Explanation
Diversity not division	Leaders promoting conflict-agility seek out diverse voices to reach better decisions that are faithfully executed without prolonged rancor.
Address conflict. Do not avoid or attack.	In the long run, a school is better off struggling with issues rather than sidestepping or suppressing conflict. Unaddressed conflict simmers below the surface.
Normalize differences without dissension.	Differences are normal and even healthy in an organization. When they are respected as part of the norm, people can express differences without discord.
Focus on the problem not the people.	Replace the tendency for personal name calling and blaming with group problem solving that meets the legitimate concerns of all stakeholders.
A process of inquiry not argument	Rather than argue over who is right, thoroughly study the problem. Brainstorm and test solutions.
Ask hard questions in a safe environment.	In a conflict-agile environment, leaders are willing to engage the school in courageous conversations about education's greatest challenges like anti-racism and equity and their specific impact on a school's practices.
Emphasis on continuous feedback not finality	People are more willing to break out of a mold if there is ongoing evaluation and the ability to revisit and revise their plans as needed.
Agreed-upon objective standards for success not subjective or individually held measures.	Disputes diminish when organization members agree on standards for success and when these standards are subject to objective evaluation.

inquiry rather than argument while exploring solutions that address mutually agreed-on needs, goals, and assessment criteria. All these characteristics serve as cornerstones of healthy, productive schools.

The elements of empathy, distributed leadership, trust, collective efficacy, and mindset all contribute to developing and sustaining a positive school culture and climate. Collaboration and empowerment overcome the negative influence of cliques, office politics, and mistrust between the school and families. Successful resolution of contentious issues creates a sense of optimism for the future and combats the presentism that focuses on getting by day to day.

As people get to know each other more deeply, sharing opinions and feelings becomes commonplace. Informal leaders emerge to address the needs of problematic situations, offering a more productive narrative to replace the us-versus-them characterization school cultures frequently ascribe to relationships with administrators. The value of surfacing assumptions and testing ideas before accepting them as fact prevails over the tendency to select solutions before thoroughly understanding the problem. Similarly, reflection becomes an accepted practice, leading to personal and professional growth.

A virtuous cycle is established in which gains become self-reinforcing: success breeds success. As schools hone their conflict-agility muscles and enact solutions to heretofore divisive issues, stakeholders feel more willing to participate in other school improvement efforts and more confident that they can achieve challenging goals. Resilience increases, with setbacks taken as a matter of course rather than being seen as insurmountable obstacles. Stories told around the school celebrate accomplishments; collective efficacy becomes enshrined in school lore. Results benefit not only relationships but also classroom instruction and student achievement.[24]

Believing that the school has the capacity, as well as the courage, to face conflict elevates expectations for performance in all aspects of school life. Ossified practices are objectively scrutinized, and stakeholders invent new practices, ceremonies, rituals, and stories that celebrate creativity and problem solving. Bland collegiality that emphasizes cordiality over the difficult task of creating a more inclusive, equitable school environment is supplanted by a collective affirmation that good enough is not an acceptable standard.

When sustained over time, the principles and practices of conflict-agility ultimately generate a critical mass that produces a more deeply committed, cohesive school, a place where collaborative work leads to greater engagement. When "the way we do things around here" includes a passionate, persistent push for improvement every day, schools can ascend to new heights of effectiveness and become productive, synergistic communities capable of surmounting seemingly intractable challenges.

CONTEMPLATING CONFLICT

Here are some questions for your consideration as you think about the contents of this chapter.

1. What is one issue your school is confronting that could benefit from a holding environment established through design thinking?
2. Which aspect of your own conflict-agility is already well developed? Which aspect needs toning?
3. Which aspect of your school's conflict-agility is already well developed? Which aspect needs toning?
4. In what ways did your views of conflict change as you read this book?

NOTES

1. Gerzon, *Leading through Conflict: How Successful Leaders Transform Differences into Opportunity* (Boston: Harvard Business School Press, 2006), 243.

2. Fullan and Quinn, *Coherence: The Right Drivers in Action for Schools, Districts, and Systems* (Thousand Oaks, CA: Corwin Press, 2016).

3. Shoho and Barnett, "The Realities of New Principals," *Journal of School Leadership* 20, no. 5 (September 2010): 561–96, doi:10.1177/105268461002000503; Hobson et al., "Issues for Early Headship—Problems and Support Strategies," National College for School Leadership, 2003, www.researchgate.net/publication/237254566_Issues_for_Early_Headship_-_Problems_and_Support_Strategies.

4. *Education Week*, "Principals, Here's How Teachers View You," October 16, 2019, www.edweek.org/leadership/principals-heres-how-teachers-view-you; Crossfield and Bourne, "Management of Interpersonal Conflict," *Insights of Anthropology* 2, no. 1 (February 24, 2018): 90–104.

5. Goksoy and Argon, "Conflicts at Schools," *Journal of Education and Training* 4, no. 4 (April 2016): 197–205; Uline, Tschannen-Moran, and Perez, "Constructive Conflict," *Teachers College Record* 105, no. 5 (June 2003): 782–815.

6. Gerzon, "*Leading through Conflict*," 97–100.

7. Heath and Heath, *Switch: How to Change Things When Change Is Hard* (New York: Broadway Books, 2010).

8. Pierce and Jussila, "Collective Psychological Ownership within the Work and Organizational Context: Construct Introduction and Elaboration," *Journal of Organizational Behavior* 31, no. 6 (August 2009): 810–34, doi:10.1002/job.628.

9. Gerzon, *Leading through Conflict*, 119.

10. Rahim, "Toward a Theory of Managing Organizational Conflict," *International Journal of Conflict Management* 13, no. 3 (March 2002): 207.

11. Gerzon, *Leading through Conflict*, 222.

12. Heifetz and Linsky, *Leadership on the Line: Staying Alive through the Dangers of Change* (Boston: Harvard Business Review Press, 2002), 102–7.

13. Runde and Flanagan, *Developing Conflict Competence: A Hands-On Guide for Leaders, Managers, Facilitators, and Teams* (San Francisco: Jossey-Bass, 2010), 2.

14. See Jehn, Greer, Levine, and Szulanski, "The Effects of Conflict Types, Dimensions, and Emergent States on Group Outcomes," *Group Decision and Negotiation* 17, no. 6 (November 2008): 465–95, doi:10.1007/s10726-008-9107-0 for a discussion of the deleterious effects of relationship conflicts.

15. As cited in Gerzon, *Leading through Conflict*, 50. The original quote may be found in David D. Chrislip, *The Collaborative Leadership Fieldbook* (San Francisco: Jossey-Bass, 2002).

16. Coggshall et al., *Generating Teaching Effectiveness: The Role of Job-Embedded Professional Learning in Teacher Evaluation* (Washington, DC: National Comprehensive Center for Teacher Quality, 2012), 4–6, https://files.eric.ed.gov/*fulltext*/ ED532776.pdf.

17. Duhigg, "What Google Learned From Its Quest to Build the Perfect Team," *New York Times*, February 25, 2016, www.nytimes.com/2016/02/28/magazine/what-google-learned-from-its-quest-to-build-the-perfect-team.html; Schneider, "Google Spent 2 Years Studying 180 Teams. The Most Successful Ones Shared These 5 Characteristics," Inc.com, July 19, 2017, www.inc.com/michael-schneider/google-thought-they-knew-how-to-create-the-perfect.html.

18. See Gerzon, *Leading through Conflict*, chaps. 4 and 6.

19. Fullan, *Leading in a Culture of Change* (San Francisco: Jossey-Bass, 2007), 9.

20. Shen, Gao, and Xia, "School as a Loosely Coupled Organization? An Empirical Examination Using National SASS 2003-04 Data," *Educational Management Administration & Leadership* 45, no. 4 (July 2017): 672, doi:10.1177/1741143216628533. The original use of the term "lubricant" appeared in Bryk et al., *Organizing Schools for Improvement: Lessons from Chicago* (Chicago: University of Chicago Press, 2009).

21. Heifetz and Linsky, *Leadership on the Line*, 51–74.

22. Khalil and Keir, "Equity-Centered Design Thinking," *Journal of Cases in Educational Leadership* 24, no. 1 (March 2021): 70–71.

23. Fairholm and Fairholm, "Leadership Amid the Constraints of Trust," *Leadership & Organization Development Journal* 21, no. 2 (March 2001): 102–9.

24. Jenni Donohoo, John Hattie, and Rachel Eells, "The Power of Collective Efficacy," *Educational Leadership* (March 2018): 41.

Bibliography

Albright, James, Jennifer Clement, and Kathryn Holmes. "School Change and the Challenge of Presentism." *Leading & Management* 18, no.1 (January 2012): 78–90.

Bacal, Robert. "Organizational Conflict—The Good, the Bad and the Ugly." *Journal for Quality and Participation* 27, no. 2 (Summer 2004): 21–22.

Baldwin, James. "As Much Truth as One Can Bear." *New York Times*, January 14, 1962.

Behal, Coonoor, and Andrew Moore. "Design Thinking and Culture Change." Mindhatch Insights. www.mindhatchllc.com/design-thinking-organizational-culture-change/.

Berg, Jill Harrison. "Leading Together/Retraining the Brain." *Educational Leadership* (May 2020): 86–87.

Brown, Daniel M. *Designing Together: The Collaboration and Conflict Management Handbook for Creative Professionals*. Indianapolis, IN: Peachpit Press, 2013.

Brown, Kellie, and Deidre Williams. "Creating Campus Teams That Perform after the Storm." *TEPSA Instructional Leader* 32, no. 3 (May 2019). www.tepsa.org/resource/creating-campus-teams-that-perform-after-the-storm.

Brown, Tim. *Change by Design*. New York: HarperCollins, 2009.

Burkus, David. "How Teams Should Make Decisions. Davidburkus.com. https://davidburkus.com/2020/11/how-teams-should-make-decisions/.

Burns, Deborah E., and Jeanne H. Purcell. "A Formative Assessment Compromise to the Grading Debate." *ASCD Express* 14, no. 31 (July 11, 2019). www.ascd.org/ascd-express/vol14/num31/a-formative-assessment-compromise-to-the-grading-debate.aspx.

Centers for Disease Control and Prevention. *Parent Engagement: Strategies for Involving Parents in School Health*. Atlanta: U.S. Department of Health and Human Services, 2012.

Chai, Wen Jia, Aini Ismafarius Abd Hamid, and Jafri Malin Abdullah. "Working Memory from the Psychological and Neurosciences Perspectives: A Review."

Frontiers of Psychology 9, no. 401 (March 27, 2018): 1–16. doi:10.3389/fpsyg.2018.00401.

Chan, Ka, Xu Huang, and Peng Ng. "Managers' Conflict Management Styles and Employee Attitudinal Outcomes: The Mediating Role of Trust." *Asia Pacific Journal of Management* 25, no. 2 (March 28, 2007): 277–95.

Cherry, Kendra. "How Does Implicit Bias Influence Behavior?" Verywellmind, September 18, 2020. www.verywellmind.com/implicit-bias-overview-4178401.

Chick, Nancy. "What Are Learning Styles?" Vanderbilt University Center for Teaching. https://cft.vanderbilt.edu/guides-sub-pages/learning-styles-preferences/.

Coburn, Cynthia E. "Shaping Teacher Sensemaking: School Leaders and the Enactment of Reading Policy." *Educational Policy* 19, no. 3 (July 2005): 476–509. doi:10.1177/0895904805276143.

Coggshall, Jane G., Claudette Rasmussen, Amy Colton, Jessica Milton, and Catherine Jacques. *Generating Teaching Effectiveness: The Role of Job-Embedded Professional Learning in Teacher Evaluation.* Washington, DC: National Comprehensive Center for Teacher Quality, 2012. https://files.eric.ed.gov/*fulltext*/ED532776.pdf .

Coleman, Peter T., Morton Deutsch, and Eric C. Marcus. *The Handbook of Conflict Resolution: Theory and Practice.* Hoboken, NJ: Wiley & Sons, 2014.

Conn, Charles, and Robert McLean. "Six Problem-Solving Mindsets for Very Uncertain Times." McKinsey Quarterly, September 15, 2020. www.mckinsey.com/business-functions/strategy-and-corporate-finance/our-insights/six-problem-solving-mindsets-for-very-uncertain-times.

Covey, Stephen R. *The 7 Habits of Highly Effective People: Personal Workbook.* New York: Simon & Schuster, 1989.

———. *The 7 Habits of Highly Effective People: Restoring the Character Ethic.* New York: Free Press, 2004.

Craven, Matt, Andy Fong, Taylor Lauricella, and Tao Tan. "The Long Haul: How Leaders Can Shift Mindsets and Behaviors to Reopen Safely." McKinsey & Company. www.mckinsey.com/business-functions/organization/our-insights/the-long-haul-how-leaders-can-shift-mindsets-and-behaviors-to-reopen-safely.

Crossfield, Devon, and Paul Andrew Bourne. "Management of Interpersonal Conflict between Principals and Teachers in Selected Secondary Schools in Bermuda." *Insights of Anthropology* 2, no. 1 (February 24, 2018): 90–104.

Cuban, Larry. "Why Change Is Often Confused with Reform: The Multilayered Curriculum." Larry Cuban on School Reform and Classroom Practice, November 19, 2018. https://larrycuban.wordpress.com/2018/12/19/why-change-is-often-confused-with-reform-the-multi-layered-curriculum/.

Dam, Rikki Frees, and Teo Yu Siang. "Design Thinking: Get a Quick Overview of the History." Interaction Design Foundation. www.interaction-design.org/literature/article/design-thinking-get-a-quick-overview-of-the-history.

———. "Stage 2 in the Design Thinking Process: Define the Problem and Interpret the Results." Interaction Design Foundation. www.interaction-design.org/literature/article/stage-2-in-the-design-thinking-process-define-the-problem-and-interpret-the-results.

De Jong, Machteld, Frans Kamsteeg, and Sierk Ybema. "Ethnographic Strategies for Making the Familiar Strange: Struggling with 'Distance' and Immersion' among Moroccan-Dutch Students." *Journal of Business Anthropology* 2, no. 2 (Fall 2013): 168–86.

De Smit, Aaron, Simon London, and Leigh Weiss. "To Unlock Better Decision Making, Plan Better Meetings." McKinsey Podcast, November 9, 2020. www.mck insey.com/business-functions/organization/our-insights/to-unlock-better-decision -making-plan-better-meetings#.

DeVos, Jordan. "Design Problems—What They Are and How to Frame Them." Toptal. www.toptal.com/designers/product-design/design-problem-statement.

Diamond, John B., and Amanda E. Lewis. *Despite the Best Intentions: How Racial Inequality Thrives in Good Schools*. Oxford: Oxford University Press, 2015.

Donohoo, Jenni, John Hattie, and Rachel Eells. "The Power of Collective Efficacy." *Educational Leadership* (March 2018): 40–44.

Drago-Severson, Eleanor, and Jessica Blum-DeStefano. *Leading Change Together: Developing Educator Capacity within Schools and Systems*. Alexandria, Virginia: Association for Supervision and Curriculum Development, 2018.

Duhigg, Charles. "What Google Learned From Its Quest to Build the Perfect Team." *New York Times*, February 25, 2016. www.nytimes.com/2016/02/28/magazine/ what-google-learned-from-its-quest-to-build-the-perfect-team.html.

Dweck, Carol. "What Having a 'Growth Mindset' Actually Means." *Harvard Business Review*, January 13, 2016. https://leadlocal.global/wp-content/uploads/2016/12/ Dweck-What-Having-a-%E2%80%9CGrowth-Mindset%E2%80%9D-Actu ally-Means-HBR.pdf.

Eddington, Sean M., Danielle Corple, Patrice M. Buzzanell, Carla Zoltowski, and Andrew Brightman. "Addressing Organizational Cultural Conflicts in Engineering with Design Thinking." *Negotiation and Conflict Management Research* 13, no. 3 (August 2020): 263–84. doi:10.1111/ncmr.12191.

Education Week. "Principals, Here's How Teachers View You." October 16, 2019. www.edweek.org/leadership/principals-heres-how-teachers-view-you.

Ehrlinger, Joyce, Wilson Readinger, and Bora Kim. "Decision-Making and Cognitive Biases." *Encyclopedia of Mental Health*. www.researchgate .net/publication/301662722_Decision-Making_and_Cognitive_Biases/link/ 59d7ee80a6fdcc2aad0650e7/download.

Fairholm, Matt R., and Gilbert W. Fairholm. "Leadership Amid the Constraints of Trust." *Leadership & Organization Development Journal* 21, no. 2 (March 2001): 102–9.

Ferrance, Eileen. *Action Research*. Providence, RI: Northeast and Islands Regional Education Laboratory, 2000.

Finklestein, Sydney, Jo Whitehead, and Andrew Campbell. *Think Again: Why Good Leaders Make Bad Decisions and How to Keep It from Happening to You*. Boston: Harvard Business Press, 2008.

Fisher, Roger, William L. Ury, and Bruce Patton. *Getting to Yes: Negotiating Agreement Without Giving In*. Second edition. New York: Penguin Books, 1991.

500womenscientists.org. "Storytelling: Central to Human Experience." https://500womenscientists.org/updates/2017/7/31/storytelling-human-experience.

Frey, Chuck. "The 7 All-Time Greatest Ideation Techniques." Innovation Management, May 30, 2013. https://innovationmanagement.se/2013/05/30/the-7-all-time -greatest-ideation-techniques/.

Fullan, Michael. *Change Forces: Probing the Depths of Educational Reform.* London: UKL Falmer Press, 1993.

———. *Leading in a Culture of Change.* San Francisco: Jossey-Bass, 2007.

———. *The New Meaning of Educational Change.* New York: Teachers College Press, 2016.

Fullan, Michael, and Joanne Quinn. *Coherence: The Right Drivers in Action for Schools, Districts, and Systems.* Thousand Oaks, CA: Corwin Press, 2016.

Gallagher, Alyssa, and Kami Thordarson. *An ASCD Study Guide for Design Thinking for School Leaders: Five Roles and Mindsets That Ignite Positive Change.* Alexandria, Virginia: Association for Supervision and Curriculum Development, 2018.

———. *Design Thinking for School Leaders: Five Roles and Mindsets That Ignite Positive Change.* Alexandria, Virginia: Association for Supervision and Curriculum Development, 2018.

Geertz, Clifford. *The Interpretation of Cultures.* New York: Basic Books, 1973.

Gerzon, Mark. *Leading Through Conflict: How Successful Leaders Transform Differences into Opportunity.* Boston: Harvard Business School Press, 2006.

Ghaffar, Abdul. "Conflict in Schools: Its Causes and Management Strategies." *Journal of Managerial Sciences* 3, no. 2 (July–December, 2009): 212–27. http://www .qurtuba.edu.pk/jms/default_files/JMS/3_2/05_ghaffar.pdf#:~:text=Conflict%20in %20Schools%3A%20Its%20Causes%20%26%20Management%20Strategies ,among%20individuals%20and%20groups%20lead%20them%20to%20conflicts.

Goksoy, Suleyman, and Turkan Argon. "Conflicts at School and Their Impact on Teachers." *Journal of Education and Training* 4, no. 4 (April 2016): 197–205.

Goodier, Steve. "Bringing Harmony to Discord." Blogspot, October 3, 2008. http:// stevegoodier.blogspot.com/2008/10/bringing-harmony-to-discord.html.

Gorman, Amanda. "The Hill We Climb." Poem Delivered at Presidential Inauguration, Washington, DC, January 20, 2021.

Heath, Chip, and Dan Heath, *Switch: How to Change Things When Change Is Hard.* New York: Broadway Books, 2010.

Heifetz, Ronald A., and Martin Linsky. *Leadership on the Line: Staying Alive through the Dangers of Change.* Boston: Harvard Business Review Press, 2002.

Heller, Rafael. "What We Know (and Think We Know) About the Learning Brain: An Interview with Tracey Tokuhama-Espinosa." *Phi Delta Kappan* (December/January 2018–2019). https://kappanonline.org/learning-brain-neuroscience-tokuhama -espinosa-heller/.

Hill, Nancy, and Diana Tyson. "Parental Involvement in Middle School: A Meta-Analytic Assessment of Strategies That Promote Achievement." *Developmental Psychology* 45, no. 3 (June 2009): 740–63.

Hobson, Andy, Ekua Brown, Pat Ashby, Wendy Keys, Caroline Sharp, and Pauline Benefield. "Issues for Early Headship—Problems and Support Strategies." National College for School Leadership, 2003. www.researchgate.net/publication/237254566_Issues_for_Early_Headship_-_Problems_and_Support_Strategies.

MasterClass. "How to Identify Cognitive Bias: 12 Examples of Cognitive Bias." November 8, 2020. www.masterclass.com/articles/how-to-identify-cognitive-bias.

Howard, Gary R. 2007. "As Diversity Grows, So Must We." *Educational Leadership*, March 16–22.

Hoy, Wayne K., and Cecil G. Miskel. *Educational Administration: Theory, Research, and Practice*. Ninth edition. New York: McGraw-Hill, 2013.

Hyatt, Michael. "Bad Decisions Don't Just Happen." Michaelhyatt.com, August 10, 2020. https://michaelhyatt.com/bad-decisions-dont-just-happen/?utm_source=feedburner&utm_medium=feed&utm_campaign=Feed%3A+michaelhyatt+%28Michael+Hyatt%29.

Interaction Design Foundation. "What Is Prototyping?" www.interaction-design.org/literature/topics/prototyping.

Isabu, M. O. "Causes and Management of School-Related Conflict." *African Educational Research Journal* 5, no. 2 (May 2017): 148–51. https://files.eric.ed.gov/fulltext/EJ1214170.pdf.

Jehn, Karen A. "A Qualitative Analysis of Conflict Types and Dimensions in Organizational Groups." *Administrative Science Quarterly* 42, no. 3 (September 1997): 530–57. doi:10.2307/2393737.

Jehn, Karen A., Lindred L. Greer, Sheen S. Levine, and Gabriel Szulanski. "The Effects of Conflict Types, Dimensions, and Emergent States on Group Outcomes." *Group Decision and Negotiation* 17, no. 6 (November 2008): 465–95. doi:10.1007/s10726-008-9107-0.

Johnson, Patsy E. "Conflict and the School Leader: Expert or Novice." www2.education.uiowa.edu/archives/jrel/spring03/Johnson_0204.htm.

Kaplan, Leslie S., and William A. Owings. *Introduction to the Principalship: Theory to Practice*. New York: Routledge, 2015.

Kappes, Andreas, Ann H. Harvey, Terry Lohrenz, P. Read Montague, and Tali Sharot. "Confirmation Bias in the Utilization of Others' Opinion Strength." *Nature Neuroscience* 23 (January, 2020): 130–37.

Keator, Timothy. "Dispute or Conflict? The Importance of Knowing the Difference." Mediate. www.mediate.com/articles/KeatorT1.cfm.

Kennedy, John F. "Re: United States Committee for UNICEF July 25, 1963." Papers of John F. Kennedy, Presidential Papers. White House Central Files. Chronological File. Series 1. President's Outgoing Executive Correspondence, Box 11, Folder "July 1963: 16–31," JFKL. www.jfklibrary.org/learn/about-jfk/life-of-john-f-kennedy/john-f-kennedy-quotations.

Kenny, Conor. "The Single Biggest Problem in Communication Is the Illusion That It Has Taken Place." *Irish Times*, November 9. www.irishtimes.com/culture/books/the-single-biggest-problem-in-communication-is-the-illusion-that-it-has-taken-place-1.4404586.

Khalil, Deena, and Meredith Kier. "Equity-Centered Design Thinking in STEM Instructional Leadership." *Journal of Cases in Educational Leadership* 24, no. 1 (March 2021): 69–85.

Knowledge@Wharton. "Why You Need a Challenge Network." https://knowledge
.wharton.upenn.edu/article/why-you-need-a-challenge-network/. https://knowl
edge.wharton.upenn.edu/article/why-you-need-a-challenge-network/.

Kowalski, Theodore J. *Effective Communication for District and School Administrators*. New York: Rowman & Littlefield, 2015.

———. *The School Superintendent: Theory, Practice, and Cases*. Third edition. Los
Angeles: Sage Publications, 2013.

Lencioni, Patrick. *The Five Dysfunctions of a Team: A Leadership Fable*. San Francisco: Jossey-Bass, 2002.

Levin, Stephanie, Kathryn Bradley, and Caitlin Scott. *Principal Turnover: Insights
from Current Principals*. Palo Alto, CA: Learning Policy Institute / Reston, VA:
National Association of Secondary School Principals, 2019. https:/learningpolicy
institute.org/product/nassp-principal-turnover-insights-brief.

Liedtka, Jeanne. "Why Design Thinking Works." *Harvard Business Review* (September–October, 2018). https://hbr.org/2018/09/why-design-thinking-works.

Liggett, Rob. "Toward a Conceptualization of Democratic Leadership in a Professional Context." *Canadian Journal of Educational Administration and Policy* 193
(2020): 115–27.

Martin, M. Jason. "'That's the Way We Do Things Around Here': An Overview of
Organizational Culture." *Electronic Journal of Academic and Special Librarianship* 7, no. 1 (2006). https://southernlibrarianship.icaap.org/content/v07n01/martin
_m01.htm.

Martines, Jamie. "For Ed-Tech Success, Why Schools Use Technology Is Just as
Important as How: A California School Group Refined Its Goals before Turning to
an Ed-Tech Company." Hechinger Report, August 3, 2016. https://hechingerreport
.org/for-ed-tech-success-why-schools-use-technology-is-just-as-important-as-how/.

Marzano, Robert J., Timothy Waters, and Brian A. McNulty. *School Leadership That
Works: From Research to Results*. Alexandria, VA: Association for Supervision and
Curriculum Development, 2005.

Mayer, Bernard. *The Dynamics of Conflict: A Guide to Engagement and Intervention*.
Second edition. San Francisco: Jossey-Bass, 2012.

Meckler, Laura, and Kate Rabinowitz. 2019. "The Changing Face of School
Integration." *Washington Post*, September 12. www.washingtonpost.com/edu
cation/2019/09/12/more-students-are-going-school-with-children-different-races
-schools-big-cities-remain-deeply-segregated/ .

Mslia, Vuyisile. "Conflict Management and School Leadership." *Journal of Communication* 3, no.1 (July 2012): 25–34.

Mujic, Julie A. 2015. "Education Reform and the Failure to Fix Inequality in America." *Atlantic*, October 29, 2015. www.theatlantic.com/education/archive/2015/10/
education-solving-inequality/412729/.

National Center for Education Statistics. *National Household Education Survey*.
Washington, DC: U.S. Department of Education, 2019. https://nces.ed.gov/
pubs2020/2020076full.pdf.

———. *National Teacher and Principal Survey*. Washington, DC: U.S. Department
of Education, 2018. https://nces.ed.gov/surveys/ntps/tables/pfs1617_fl03_p1n.asp.

National Institute of Mental Health Information Resource Center. *Five Things You Should Know About Stress*. Washington, DC: U.S. Department of Health and Human Services, 2019. www.nimh.nih.gov/health/publications/stress/.

National PTA. "The Center for Family Engagement." www.pta.org/center-for-family -engagement.

Northeast and Islands Regional Educational Laboratory. *The Diversity Kit: An Introductory Resource for Social Change in Education, Part I: Human Development*. Providence, RI: LAB at Brown University, 2002. www.brown.edu/academics/ed ucation-alliance/sites/brown.edu.academics.education-alliance/files/publications/ diversitykit.pdf.

Olson, Robert Wallace. *The Art of Creative Thinking*. New York: Barnes & Noble, 1980.

Patrick, Kayla, Allison Socol, and Ivy Morgan. *Inequities in Advanced Coursework: What's Driving Them and What Leaders Can Do*. The Education Trust, 2020. https:// edtrustmain.s3.us-east-2.amazonaws.com/wp-content/uploads/2014/09/08183916/ Inequities-in-Advanced-Coursework-Whats-Driving-Them-and-What-Leaders -Can-Do-January-2019.pdf.

Patterson, Kerry, Joseph Grenny, Ron McMillan, and Al Switzler. *Crucial Conversations: Tools for Talking When Stakes Are High*. New York: McMillan Books, 2012.

Pentland, Alex. 2012. "The New Science of Building Great Teams." *Harvard Business Review*. https://hbr.org/2012/04/the-new-science-of-building-great-teams.

Pierce, Jon L., and Iiro Jussila. "Collective Psychological Ownership Within the Work and Organizational Context: Construct Introduction and Elaboration. *Journal of Organizational Behavior* 31, no. 6 (August 2009): 810–34. doi:10.1002/job.628.

Rahim, M. Afzalur. "Toward a Theory of Managing Organizational Conflict." *International Journal of Conflict Management* 13, no. 3 (March 2002): 206–35.

Ramsey, Robert D. *How to Say the Right Thing Every Time: Communicating Well with Students, Staff, Parents, and the Public*. Second edition. Thousand Oaks, CA: Corwin, 2009.

Riddle, Thomas. "Improving Schools Through Design Thinking." Edutopia, February 3, 2016. www.edutopia.org/blog/improving-schools-through-design-thinking -thomas-riddle.

Rosenholz, Susan J. *Teachers' Workplace: The Social Organization of Schools*. New York: Longman, 1989.

Rubio, Enrique. "Solving Team's Conflict with Design Thinking." LinkedIn, June 8, 2016. www.linkedin.com/pulse/solving-teams-conflicts-design-thinking-enrique -rubio.

Rui, Ning. "Four Decades of Research on the Effects of Detracking Reform: Where Do We Stand?—A Systematic Review of the Evidence." *Journal of Evidence-Based Medicine* 2, no. 3 (August 2009): 164–83.

Runde, Craig E., and Tim A. Flanagan. *Becoming a Conflict Competent Leader: How You and Your Organization Can Manage Conflict Effectively*. San Francisco: Jossey-Bass, 2007.

———. *Building Conflict Competent Teams*. San Francisco: Jossey-Bass, 2008.

————. *Developing Conflict Competence: A Hands-On Guide for Leaders, Managers, Facilitators, and Teams*. San Francisco: Jossey-Bass, 2010.

————. "How Teams Can Capitalize on Conflict." *Strategy and Leadership* 37, no. 1 (January 2009). doi:10.1108/10878570910926025.

Ryan, James. *Leading Diverse Schools*. New York: Kluwer Academic Publishers, 2003.

Sagor, Richard. *Guiding School Improvement with Action Research*. Alexandria, VA: Association for Supervision and Curriculum Development, 2000.

Salzburg, Sharon. "Quotes." Goodreads. www.goodreads.com/author/quotes/17208. Sharon_Salzberg?page=3.

Schneider, Michael. "Google Spent 2 Years Studying 180 Teams. The Most Successful Ones Shared These 5 Characteristics." Inc.com, July 19, 2017. www.inc.com/michael-schneider/google-thought-they-knew-how-to-create-the-perfect.html.

Shen, Jianping, Xingyuan Gao, and Jiangang Xia. (2017). "School as a Loosely Coupled Organization? An Empirical Examination Using National SASS 2003–2004 Data." *Educational Management Administration & Leadership* 45, no. 4 (July 2017): 657–81. doi:10.1177/1741143216628533.

Shoho, Alan R., and Bruce G. Barnett. "The Realities of New Principals: Challenges, Joys, and Sorrows." *Journal of School Leadership* 20, no. 5 (September 2010): 561–96. doi:10.1177/105268461002000503.

Solly, Meilan. "158 Resources to Understand Racism in America." *Smithsonian Magazine*, June 4. www.smithsonianmag.com/history/158-resources-understanding-systemic-racism-america-180975029/.

Spencer, John. "The Launch Cycle: A K–12 Design Thinking Framework." https://spencerauthor.com/the-launch-cycle/.

Spillane, James P., Brian J. Reiser, and Todd Reimer. "Policy Implementation and Cognition: Reframing and Refocusing Implementation Research." *Review of Educational Research* 72, no. 3 (September 2002): 387–431. doi:10.3102/00346543072003387.

Stronge, James H., Holly B. Richard, and Nancy Catano. *Qualities of Effective Principals*. Alexandria, VA: Association for Supervision and Curriculum Development, 2008.

Tatum, Beverly Daniel. "Color Blind or Color Conscious?" School Superintendents Association. www.aasa.org/SchoolAdministratorArticle.aspx?id=14892.

Thien, Lee Min, and N. A. Razak. "A Proposed Framework of School Organization from Open System and Multilevel Organization Theories." *World Applied Sciences Journal* 20, no. 6 (2012): 889–99. doi:10.5829/idosi.wasj.2012.20.06.2016.

Tschannen-Moran, Megan. *Trust Matters: Leadership for Successful Schools*. Hoboken, NJ: Wiley Publishing, 2014.

Tyack, David, and William Tobin. "The 'Grammar' of Schooling: Why Has It Been So Hard to Change?" *American Educational Research Journal* 31, no. 3 (Fall 1994): 453–79.

Uline, Cynthia, Megan Tschannen-Moran, and Lynne Perez. "Constructive Conflict: How Controversy Can Contribute to School Improvement." *Teachers College Record* 105, no. 5 (June 2003): 782–815.

University College London. "Energy Demands Limit Our Brains' Information Processing Capacity." ScienceDaily, August 3, 2020. www.sciencedaily.com/releases/2020/08/200803140046.htm.

VandenBos, Gary R., ed. *American Psychological Association Dictionary of Psychology*. Second edition. Washington, DC: American Psychological Association, 2015.

Wallace Foundation. *The School Principal as Leader: Guiding Schools to Better Teaching and Learning*. New York: Wallace Foundation, 2013. www.wallace foundation.org/knowledge-center/pages/the-school-principal-as-leader-guiding -schools-to-better-teaching-and-learning.aspx.

Wang, Fei, Katrina Pollock, and Cameron Hauseman. "School Principals' Job Satisfaction: The Effects of Work Intensification." *Canadian Journal of Educational Administration and Policy* 185 (2018): 73–90.

Weick, Karl E. "Educational Organizations as Loosely Coupled Systems." *Administrative Science Quarterly* 21, no. 1 (March 1976): 1–19.

Wells, Amy Stuart, Lauren Fox, and Diana Cordova-Cobo. *How Racially Diverse Schools and Classrooms Can Benefit All Students*. Century Foundation, 2016. https://tcf.org/content/report/how-racially-diverse-schools-and-classrooms-can-benefit-all-students/?session=1.

Whitaker, Todd. *Dealing with Difficult Teachers*. Second edition. Larchmont, NY: Eye on Education, 2002.

Zwilling, Martin. "Ten Top Attributes Elevate Design Thinking Leaders." Alley-Watch, December 6, 2017. www.alleywatch.com/2017/12/10-top-attributes-elevate -design-thinking-leaders/.

Index

About the Authors

Robert Feirsen has served as an assistant principal, principal, deputy superintendent, and superintendent of schools. He is currently chair of the Education Department, College of Arts and Sciences, at New York Institute of Technology, where he teaches courses in school leadership in addition to his administrative responsibilities. Dr. Feirsen also taught at the elementary, middle, and high school levels as a social studies and special education teacher before moving into supervisory roles. Dr. Feirsen's work has been published in professional journals, magazines, and books. With Seth Weitzman, he is the coauthor of *How to Get the Teaching Job You Want*, a guide to the job search process in education. Dr. Feirsen has also presented at international, national, and regional conferences on topics including teacher and school leader hiring and retention, school principal–school counselor relationships, district leadership, school culture, and design thinking. He holds degrees from Stony Brook University, Queens College (CUNY), and Fordham University, where he earned his doctorate in school administration and supervision.

Seth Weitzman has served twenty-seven years as a principal following three years as an assistant principal, totaling three decades of school building administration, all in middle schools. He has held leadership positions in professional associations and professional learning networks at the district, county, and state levels. Additionally, he is the author of articles in national publications including *Educational Leadership* and *American Association for Middle Level Education Magazine*. In addition to coauthoring *How to Get the Teaching Job You Want* with Dr. Feirsen, Dr. Weitzman has presented at numerous state and national conferences, specializing in teacher and administrator hiring and retention and conflict remediation. Since retiring from public school administration, he has embarked on a second career as an adjunct professor in Mercy College's Education Leadership program. He began his career teaching in a diverse set of suburban and urban schools in the New York tri-state area including five years in New York City schools. He holds a doctorate from Teachers College, Columbia University.

Further Praise for *From Conflict to Collaboration: A School Leader's Guide to Unleashing Conflict's Problem-Solving Power*

"Drs. Feirsen and Weitzman have put together a book that helps to address how school principals and other school administrators can work through conflict, both our internal conflicts and the conflicts that happen in schools. Reframing conflict with the mindset that conflict leads to collaboration and conversation is not only a positive twist on conflict but a healthy twist on conflict, too. I found myself applying the ideas in *From Conflict to Collaboration* while I was reading. *From Conflict to Collaboration* is a great book to help any school administrator who is working through conflict, and the 'who' is everyone."

—Jay Posick, principal, Merton, Wisconsin, and coauthor,
Principals in Action: Redefining the Role

"Drs. Feirsen and Weitzman have brought together the essential ingredients of success for every administrator of educational programs. I wish this was available when I was in the throes of my administrative career struggling daily to go from *Conflict to Collaboration*. We intend on using it with our aspiring administrators at my college immediately. It is a bit cliché to say this has it all but in reality, this book offers new insights, synthesizes age old techniques and gets directly to the heart of complicated matters in a smooth and easy to read manner, it truly does have it all. I recommend this to all current administrators because a thorough read of this book will make your job much more untroublesome and I believe it will improve your chances of creating a place of joy in your work environment. For aspiring administrators, I would highly recommend you get this book immediately. You will eliminate many unnecessary reads since this treasure chest by two enormously successful administrators is a practical how-to for creating a successful organization. This book is destined to be a classic must read for generations of educators to com—BRAVO!"

—Rick McMahon, coordinator, Iona College
Education Department Graduate Programs

"Feirsen and Weitzman's novel approach to conflict as an opportunity for constructive change has much to offer school leaders. Their focus on inward Design Thinking will enable leaders to address the systems issues that lead to outward conflict, prevent spiraling downward, and develop solutions that work for all. Filled with practical suggestions and steeped in research, their book will assist in the development of conflict-agility which will lead to school improvement and powerful dynamic positive cultures."

—Joe Famularo, EdD, superintendent, Bellmore,
New York Public Schools and author of *IOU Life Leadership*

"This book offers a framework that empowers a school community to make better decisions resulting in a call to action, moving from hopes and dreams to reality. By taking the time to gather information about what people are thinking, feeling, saying, and doing will increase capacity for problem-solving in the application of the Design Thinking process. Designing prototypes (for example, rubrics in Standard Based Grading) and testing them with feedback gathered at each stage, will allow teachers 'permission' to fail as they strive to develop the best possible learning experiences for students. Viewing obstacles through a lens of opportunity for improvement will lead to greater collective efficacy among PLC teams."

—Brenda Vatthauer, principal, Hutchinson, Minnesota